Christiane Bröcker / Babette Schröder

111 Places
in Stockholm
That You Must
Not Miss

emons:

Bibliographical information of the Deutsche Nationalbibliothek
The Deutsche Nationalbibliothek lists this publication
in the Deutsche Nationalbibliografie; detailed bibliographical
data are available on the internet at http://dnb.d-nb.de.

© Emons Verlag GmbH
All rights reserved
© Photographs: Christiane Bröcker, except:
The Museum Flat: Alexander Mahmoud, Stockholm Stadmuset;
Årsta Islands and Tea House: Agneta Skoglar;
Carl Eldh's Studio:Carl Hjelte
Design: Eva Kraskes, based on a design
by Lübekke | Naumann | Thoben
Maps: altancicek.design, www.altancicek.de
English translation: Kathleen Becker
Printing and binding: Grafisches Centrum Cuno, Calbe
Printed in Germany 2014
ISBN 978-3-95451-459-5
First edition

Did you enjoy it? Do you want more?
Join us in uncovering new places around the world on:
www.111places.com

Foreword

Until we started researching this book we thought Stockholm was an incredibly beautiful city, one that would charm us time and again with its unique light, venerable buildings, wealth of water and its sheer expanse.

Now, after spending weeks walking through the city centre from one end to the other in sun, rain and snow storms, with expeditions leading into numerous suburbs and stumbling into more than one unusual situation during our hunt for a new insiders' tip, our image of the city has changed.

We have discovered far more than 111 interesting, mysterious, amusing, eccentric and romantic sites that mirror the stories behind them. Before we started on this endeavour we thought: Stockholm is beautiful. Now we know: Stockholm is beautiful, idiosyncratic and sexy!

Sports aficionados, children, gamblers, art lovers and culture vultures, adventurous souls, friends of nature and foodies, nostalgic souls and dancing folk will find a variety of highly original places. Places where people – as Pippi Longstocking might say – create a world to their own liking. Places that have something on offer for everyone. So it's our heartfelt wish that you will thoroughly enjoy this discovery tour!

111 Places

2

1 The Adat Jeshurun Synagogue

The story of a miraculous rescue

From the outside it's not at all obvious what treasure lies hidden in the simple yellow building in Riddargatan. The second floor of the Jewish school located here houses the Orthodox synagogue of Adat Jeshurun. The furnishings with its pretty prayer benches, their outsides painted with tender green leaf tendrils, arrived here after a long journey. They once belonged to a synagogue in Hamburg's Heinrich Barth Street. Occupying the second floor of an equally inconspicuous residential house, the synagogue escaped destruction by the Nazis, who simply overlooked it during the Night of Broken Glass. However, Joseph Carlebach, Chief Rabbi at the time, had the premonition that the synagogue would sooner or later fall victim to the pogrom and asked his friend Hans Lehmann in Stockholm for help. The wealthy businessman had already emigrated to Sweden in the early 1930s. Carlebach wanted to save the furnishings of the synagogue and get them to Stockholm by boat. Lehmann agreed to pay the transport costs and promised to look after the precious cargo.

In boxes labelled "Wood and Household Goods" the magnificent torah shrine and the masterfully carved prayer benches did reach Stockholm's industrial port in spring 1939, if heavily damaged. Workers loyal to the Nazis had smashed up parts of the cargo and carved swastikas into the wood. Still, Hans Lehmann kept his word and commissioned restorers from Stockholm's National Museum with repairing the damage. Today, the torah shrine is intact again and in regular use.

Joseph Carlebach and his family were deported in 1941 to the concentration camp Jungfernhof near Riga, where he was shot dead a few months later. The building in Heinrich Barth Street was destroyed in a 1943 air raid.

Address Riddargatan 5, 11435 Stockholm-Östermalm | Public transport Östermalmstorg (T-bana 13, 14) | Opening times Visiting the synagogue with a group is possible by appointment. Contact the Great Synagogue: info@jfst.se | Tip Also well worth seeing, the Great Synagogue on Wahrendorffsgatan may be visited between June and August Monday to Thursday at 11am and 1pm, Fridays at 11am (www.jfst.se).

2 The Aeter & Essence Factory

A paradise of herbs and spices

Do you know this game where you have to recognise foodstuffs by their scent – blindfolded? It's an interesting experience. The aroma seems familiar and yet is difficult to pin down. The same thing happens when stepping into the small "Aeter & Essence Factory". A fascinating blend of delicious aromas excites the sense of smell. Perhaps the large bright-red tin cans on the shelves sporting the words Coriander, Cumin or Fänkål in curved letters can help identify them?

The factory, which apart from essences of every kind also sells hundreds of spices and a wealth of spice blends, is the oldest of its kind in Sweden. It was founded in 1887 by Adolf Fredrik Lilieblad, who extracted essences and concentrates from fruit, berries and herbs and sold them to industry as well as bakeries. To this day most items are prepared according to the original recipes – naturally without preservatives.

In 1889 Lilieblad opened the shop which to this day has remained unchanged, extending the range of products by adding spices and herbs. At the end of the 19th century offerings in the sector were fairly limited in Sweden, and soon enough Stockholm's housewives spread the news amongst themselves about this shop in Wallingatan selling high-quality spices at low prices. Meanwhile managed in the fourth generation by the same family it looks exactly the way it did 100 years ago. Goods are still weighed using vintage mechanical scales and even the cash register is still the original.

Alongside ingredients for baking and cooking the factory also offers some interesting blends for home-made spirits, including spice mixtures for brandy from 19th-century recipes. These bear interesting names, such as "Black Widow", particularly suitable for fans of liquorice. The only risk: "You just can't stop," warns the shop assistant.

Address Wallingatan 14, 11124 Stockholm-Norrmalm | Public transport Hötorget
(T-bana 17, 18, 19) | Opening times Mon–Fri 10am–6pm, Sat 10am–3pm | Tip Grill
(Drottninggatan 89), a bar & restaurant, which stands out through its original and
ever-changing furnishings (Mon–Fri 11.15am–2pm and from 5pm, Sat from 4pm,
Sun from 3pm).

3__The Anna Lindh Memorial
The end of the people's politician

If the assasination of Anna Lindh had taken place at a public place she would probably be commemorated there. In the event, the knife attack which wounded the popular politician on 10 September 2003 so badly that she died from her wounds the next morning happened in the women's section of the NK department store. It is understandable that the popular shopping mecca was not overly keen to remind visitors of the sad chapter in its history.

Thus, the city commemorates the then foreign minister with an unpretentious three-metre column of green glass on the steps of the Medborgarhus. Particularly in summer, the Medborgarplats with its beer gardens and restaurants is a popular place. It is also often the point of departure for demonstrations. And this is also the spot where the charismatic politician held what was to be her last public speech on 9 September 2003.

In 2001 she had gained international reputation as chairperson of the Council of the European Union. Lindh worked towards preventing the Iraq War and promoted the introduction of the euro in Sweden. The Medborgarplatsen saw her last attempt to convince her fellow citizens of the advantages of leaving the national currency. Still, on 5 September 56 per cent of Swedes cast their vote in favour of maintaining the Swedish crown.

When the perpetrator was arrested 14 days after the attack, he claimed that voices in his head had pushed him to do it. Whilst his legal accountability was controversial, he was finally condemned to serve a life sentence by the appellate court of last resort.

Following the the murder of prime minister Olof Palme in 1986, the brutal attack on Anna Lindh once more shook the country to its core. One year after Lindh's death, the "Svenska Dagbladet" wrote: "When the murderer fled from the scene, he took with him the last hope of a peaceful safe society."

Utrikesminister
ANNA LINDH
höll sitt sista tal
på trappan till
Medborgarhuset
9 september 2003

Address Medborgarplatsen, 11872 Stockholm-Södermalm | **Public transport** Medborgarplatsen (T-bana 17, 18, 19, bus 59, 66, 193, 194, 195, 791, 794) | **Tip** On the other side of the Götgatan is a skatepark, where youngsters engage in their manoeuvers, some of them quite spectacular.

4_Anna Lindhagen's Little Garden

... commemorates the pioneer of allotment gardening

In Stigbergsgatan, opposite the house with the number 30, a small set of steps leads down to a pretty garden with an old-fashioned gazebo. It might look like a private plot, but passers-by are welcome to take a seat on the bench around the splendid maple tree and enjoy the fine views of the water, the Gröna Lund fun park and Skeppsholmen island.

The garden is named after the Social Democrat politician and women's rights activist Anna Lindhagen, who lived below this plot of land in Fjällgatan. Working the soil of the steep mountain, she bedded out wild plants from the Schärgarten (some 30,000 small islands off Stockholm). It is a fitting gesture for Anna Lindhagen, who worked for the preservation of Old Södermalm and is considered a pioneer of the Swedish allotment gardening movement. Her commitment to this cause can be traced back to a 1903 visit to Copenhagen, where she visited an inner-city colony of allotment gardens.

In the wake of industrialisation, the population of Stockholm had increased substantially. Anna Lindhagen wanted to provide less wealthy people with no garden of their own with the opportunity of relaxing within the city and of growing their own vegetables. In 1904 she managed to convince the Royal Administration of Djurgården to introduce public allotments in Stockholm. Renting a plot of land she founded the city's first allotment colony on Norra Djurgården. In 1905, when the association gave themselves their first administration, the dynamic politician took the helm. There were strict rules that all allotment holders had to respect if they didn't want to face the cancellation of their contract. Lindhagen had strict ideas about what the individual plots should look like, even defining which flowers she preferred to see planted. This earned her the grudge of the male plot owners, unhappy to take orders from a woman.

Address Opposite Stigbergsgatan 30, 11628 Stockholm-Södermalm | **Public transport** Medborgarplatsen (T-bana 17, 18, 19); Ersta sjukhus (bus 2, 53, 71, 96) | **Tip** Discover the Greta Garbo Square with a small monument of the diva only five minutes away on foot, at the corner of Katarina Bangata and Södermannagatan. It is lit up by a spotlight in the evening, so by standing on the star in the ground you will be illuminated and become a star in your own right.

5 Antikt, Gammalt & Nytt

Where any woman turns into a princess

At the heart of a neighbourhood dominated mainly by the shopping meccas of major designer labels, this charming gem comes as a complete surprise. Upon entering this narrow shop visitors are surrounded by a pleasant powdery scent carrying them away into another world. The rows upon rows of glass cabinets hold mainly jewellery and ladies' hats for any occasion and every price range. Everything seems to sparkle and glitter.

Light-footed Mats and Tore weave their way through the narrow aisles, finding a kind word for each and every customer. After a while one gets used to constantly being in the way somewhere and starts twisting and turning around customers and display cases with as much verve as the two owners.

Only now do the eyes start to make out individual objects amongst this colourful glitter fest and appreciate the lovingly assembled decor. The glass cabinets are topped by female busts, all wearing unusual hats, sunglasses and jewellery. Some have been wrapped in a corset or fur stola. Jewellery is everywhere, laid out or dangling off something, from cheap ear studs to the one-off antique ring. In between, putti-shaped salt and pepper shakers, unusual Christmas decorations (all year round naturally) and images of saints can be found.

Mats and Tore buy whatever they like. Observing them for a while is a lesson in what passion looks like. When four decades ago they hit upon a depot with all kinds of stuff from the 1940s, they knew they had found their vocation. Both chucked in their jobs and have been looking for unusual pieces at fairs or at film and theatre venues, but also at household clearances all over the world ever since.

Who they sell to remains secret. It doesn't really matter, here any customer is a princess. However, we can safely reveal that in the run-up to court events business can and does soar.

Address Mäster Samuelsgatan 11, 11144 Stockholm-Normalm | **Public transport** Östermalmstorg (T-bana13 and 15) | **Opening times** Mon–Fri 11am–6pm, Sat 12 midday–4pm | **Tip** The unusual multi-car park standing at the corner of Samuels-gatan and Regeringsgatan dates from the 1960s. At first glance it seems the concrete facade simply bears an interesting pattern. Looking more closely reveals that the numbers mark individual storeys. They are mirrored, which leads to this unusual visual effect.

6 _ The Aronsberg Cemetery

Forgotten between high-rises

Tall appartment blocks line the Alströmergatan. All of a sudden, a yawning gap appears amongst them. Surrounded by a cast-iron fence, various fairly askew headstones bearing Hebrew letters stand in no particular order. In their midst a beech tree spreads its protective branches across this calm place. While there is nowhere any indication relating to it, this is the oldest Jewish cemetery in Stockholm. If it wasn't a Jewish cemetery it would probably have had to make way for another high-rise. But the Jewish faith forbids removing grave stones and mortal remains.

The cemetery takes its name from Aaron Isaak, a German merchant and seal engraver who in 1774 was the first Jewish person to arrive in Stockholm. Having manufactured some seals for Swedish officers back in Germany and hearing that his profession was in demand in Sweden, he headed north.

Isaak was lucky to be made the protégé of the governor of Stockholm, which facilitated obtaining work and residence permits. Finally, King Gustav III allowed him to invite over the ten Jewish men necessary for a complete religious service. Moreover, he was allowed to employ a rabbi.

This marked the birth of Stockholm's Jewish community. The permission to open a Jewish cemetery followed in 1776. But those rights didn't come for free. The King demanded 2000 silver crowns for the privilege, the equivalent of about 20 annual salaries at the time.

The Jewish community soon grew to 150 members, and differences emerged. Isaak was considered quite authoritarian, with a controversial leadership style. In 1787 an opposition formed, the members of which decided to establish their own cemetery. So, only eleven years after the first Jewish cemetery, a second one was established nearby – the Kronoberg Cemetery.

Address Alströmergatan 22–34, 11247 Stockholm-Kungsholmen | Public transport Frid-hemsplan (T-bana 10, 11, 17, 18, 19); Arbetargatan (bus 49) | Opening times Open daily, all year round | Tip The Kronoberg Cemetery lies just around the corner in the western part of the park of the same name. This occupies a lovely position up on a hill, the highest point in the area.

7_ The Årsta Islands
It is the nightingale and not the lark

Particularly in late May and early June it's worth taking a stroll or a bike trip in the evening or the early hours of the day on the Årstabron railway bridge between Södermalm and Årsta. After coming to a stop more or less in the middle of the structure and waiting for the occasional train to have rumbled by there is the opportunity of enjoying a wonderful birdsong chorus.

Below the bridge you'll spot an island in the Årstaviken. 18th-century maps still show three islets separate from each other but the land uplift made them merge. However, the individual characteristics of the original islets are still distinguishable: Lillholmen in the east has large expanses, Bergholmen has a rocky hillock, and Åhlholmen in the west features a wooden house dating back to 1737. Serving as a summer residence at the time it comprised an orangery as well as an orchard.

Since 1886 the island has been in the possession of the city of Stockholm. The former estate house is a guesthouse and meeting centre today; other than that the island is uninhabited and only accessible by boat. Plans are for a small footbridge to lead across from Södermalm, but this is controversial as it would pose a danger for the habitat.

Over the past decades a natural biotope developed due to the island's remote location. Various songbirds including wren, nightingale and blackcap have become naturalised here, all known for their strong singing voice. The tawny owl too is said to be nesting in the trees.

The songs of the nightingale in particular makes a visit worthwhile. Its song is extraordinarily varied, complex and simply beautiful. When the males look for a female breeding partner in the spring they sing loudly and clearly at night. During breeding season in June they delight passers-by in the daytime too.

Address Årsta Holmar, 11842 Stockholm-Årsta | Public transport Tanto (bus 43) Årstagård (bus 160) | Tip Another lovely option is to approach the island by kayak, listening to the birds from the water. Kajaks are rented out by "Elite Marina", Årstaängsvägen 11 (tel. +468/40020041).

8 Årsta torg

Where the architects themselves picked up a paint brush

The large square with the small row of colourful houses, a cinema and library seems a bit odd. Some would say ugly even. Few people know that this is the first ever Swedish neighbourhood community centre, today enjoying listed status.

It was still wartime when in 1943 the city of Stockholm commissioned the architect brothers Erik and Thore Ahlsén with laying out the square. Following the example of English "neighbourhood units", the brief was to create an autonomous centre with services of all kinds, communal facilities and flats outside the city centre. The director of town planning at the time, Sven Markelius, was a strong proponent of this concept, aiming to give life to the suburbs, promoting mutual exchange, as opposed to the dormitory towns – this was meant as a blueprint for a living democracy.

In 1944 the city gave the green light for the design developed by the Ahlsén brothers; however, due to the war construction only started in 1946. The resulting complex had flats, shops, a library, hobby and vocational training rooms, a cinema and a meeting centre. When the time came to paint the facades, the Ahlséns themselves picked up a paintbrush. Whether the reason was that the money was starting to run out or that professional painter and decorator firms refused to carry out the architects' specifications is not really known. According to the brothers the act was aimed at promoting discussion and exchange of ideas amongst the residents. On 1 November 1953 the complex was solemnly inaugurated.

Unfortunately the concept was not successful. Rents for the shared facilities were too high. Most residents worked in the city centre and only got home in the evening. Today the square still appears a bit abandoned, the benches alongside the fountain remaining empty. However, in one thing the architects were successful: their facade design is still a topic for conversation today.

Address Årsta torg, 12054 Stockholm-Årsta | Public transport Årsta torg (bus 160, 164, 168) | Tip An old estate house, Årsta Gård stands at Svärdlångsvägen 14. Martha Helena Reenstierna, who became famous through her diaries under the name of Årsta Fru resided here in the 19th century. They say that her spirit still haunts the garden at night.

9__ The Artists' House

Long live art

The inscription above the fine old oak door sounds like a motto for the Konstnärhus: "Ars longa, vita brevis – Life is short, art is long." It's a near miracle actually that this house, which was established at the end of the 19th century out of a protest movement against the Royal Academy of Fine Arts has lasted to this day. Swedish artists, having discovered their love of open-air painting during study trips to Paris, no longer wanted anything to do with the salon and studio painting still prevalent in Sweden at the time. Eventually, in 1897 the artists' associations "Svenska Konstnärernas Förening" (SKF) and "Konstnärsklubben" (KK) came together in an attempt to reconcile the various art movements with each other and to create a house for all artists.

A plot on Östermalm was purchased and architect Ludwig Petersen commissioned to build the house. The pretty facade of the listed building is heavily influenced by the Moorish style popular at the time.

The impressively painted vaulted staircase inside, the bannister, down to the door handles – everything was designed by artists, as befits a house of this kind.

An indication of the fact that the associates didn't always agree on artistic concepts and the best way to organise the house are the 6000 tablecloths the artists used to draw caricatures of each other during association meetings. The first were of fabric but the restaurant owner quickly changed over to paper. One of those valuable specimens can be admired in the staircase.

The five-storey building belongs to the two associations to this day and thus to the artists. They use it to showcase their work in public exhibitions and to hold meetings and round-table discussions. Moreover, the associations award grants and since 1938 have sustained an aid fund for elderly and needy artists.

Address Smålandsgatan 7, 11146 Stockholm-Östermalm | **Public transport** Östermalmstorg (T-bana 13, 14); Norrmalmstorg (bus 2, 47, 55, 69, 71, 76) | **Opening times** Tue–Thu 12 noon–5pm, Fri–Sat 12 noon–4pm | **Tip** The lower floor of the house is occupied by the "Konstnärsbar" restaurant. The furnishings, well worth seeing, date back to the 1930s, when various artists designed the impressive walls.

10_ The Bee Hives

Industrious bees populating the roofs of Stockholm

Rosendals Trädgård, the former orangery of Rosendal Palace on Djurgården, is a public garden with fruit trees, flowers, herbs and organically grown vegetables. The idyllic garden café serves homemade cakes. Visitors strolling through the apple yard in summer will discover a row of bee hives painted light blue at the edge of the lawn. So what's so special about them? Those are bees one can adopt!

Biologists Karolina Lisslö and Josefina Oddsberg launched their project to call attention to the fact that the world-wide bee population has declined dramatically, and at the same time wanted to offer some practical help.

In Sweden some 30 per cent of the bee and bumblebee species are extinct. If you think about it, every third bite we take is the result of a bee's pollination. Without them there would be no fruit or vegetables and the production of meat and milk would involve considerably higher effort and costs.

Since the turn of the millennium a species of mite has caused a drastic increase in the death of bee populations. Monocultures and the use of herbicides also play their part in reducing suitable habitats for bees, particularly in rural areas. In contrast, urban gardens, parks, balconies and terraces offer a varied selection of plants for bees.

This was the starting point for "Bee Urban". The company distributes bee hives – usually on roofs – in all parts of the greater Stockholm urban area. The whole project is financed by sponsors. Thus, companies have the oppourtunity of sponsoring a bee hive and whilst "Bee Urban" guarantees upkeep and maintenance, the honey reverts to the sponsor. A pretty designer bee hive set up on a sponsors' company grounds is a nice public relations vehicle to underline their commitment to the environment. Alternatively they might wish to fund a bee hive elsewhere, say, on school grounds.

Address Rosendalsterrassen 12, 11521 Stockholm-Djurgården | Public transport Bellmansro (tram 7) | Tip Fancy adopting some bees? Take a look at www.beeurban.se. Located next door, Rosendal Palace is open for visitors from 1 June to1 September (Tue–Sun 12 midday, 1pm, 2pm and 3pm).

11_ The Biology Museum
Experiencing nature in a different way

This man had a vision. Some would say he was possessed. The Museum of Biology represents the realisation of a dream held by taxidermist and amateur zoologist Gustaf Kolthoff. Kolthoff wanted to show visitors the most authentic approach to the fauna of Sweden. With this in mind, he had architect Agi Lindegren design a building in the style of a stave church, a typically Scandinavian wooden structure in the Middle Ages.

A tall round exhibition hall forms the centre of the museum. This encompasses a 360-degree diorama with a painted horizon. The well-known Swedish animal painter Bruno Liljefors created an impressive ocean scenery here with rocks blending into a forest scenery.

The painted background is complemented by an appropriately decorated foreground: a sandy beach with real rocks and trees, pastures and caves. Set everywhere against this very realistic-looking backdrop there are numerous stuffed animals on exhibition: elks, a family of foxes, a bear and a beaver. A pair of swans sit on the edge of a small pond, while scores of seabirds throng the beach and rocks. A sea eagle observes the scene from his throne atop a tree. There are no explanatory signs to disturb this nature experience. However, the entrance desk offers relevant information for interested visitors.

The idea that Gustaf Kolthoff killed and prepared all the animals exhibited here with his own hands might seem a bit spooky to some, but on the other hand holds a certain fascination, too. The hobby zoologist must have been an indefatigable hunter to obtain the exhibits for his museum. Always striving for the utmost authenticity with the exhibited landscape, he even brought back with him the natural environment of the hunted animal into the museum. The sea eagle for instance occupies his original nest.

Address Hazeliusporten 2, 11521 Stockholm-Djurgården | Public transport Nordiska museet/Vasa (tram 7, bus 44) | Opening times Oct–March: Tue–Fri 12 midday–3pm, Sat–Sun 10am–3pm; April–Sep.: daily 11am–4pm | Tip Not even five minutes away on foot is the "Estonia" monument, consisting of granite walls 2.5m/over 8ft tall and arranged in a triangle. The monument bears the engraved names of the 852 people who died in the 1994 ferry disaster.

12__ The Birger Jarl Oak

A tree with a strong will for life

At nearly 800 years of age, this tree is as old as the city of Stockholm. Whether this is the reason for naming it after city founder Birger Jarl at some point in time or whether it was the man himself who planted it remains unclear. The tree stands in a lonely spot next to the city motorway, whilst its equally aged sisters are all located in parks on Djurgården.

In the 17th and 18th centuries, the oak stood in Hornsberg's palace park which used to occupy this spot. In 1930, when it already boasted an impressive circumference of six metres (nearly 20 feet), it was still standing on a peaceful pasture between Kristineberg Palace and Hornsberg's allotment gardens.

Over the following decades residential developments went up around it and in the 1960s the urban motorway was built right in front. The road was specifically laid out to go around the tree, which is why it describes a little curve here.

While not situated in a nature reserve the oak enjoys a similar degree of protection. And despite being hollow inside and filled with concrete since the late 1950s there is still life in this tree. Two of its branches sport green leaves.

There is no sign telling the occasional passer-by why this oak is so special, and the gnarly trunk is protected only by a paltry construction fence. Paying a visit to the old lady involves a bit of hard work, as she is not exactly easy to find.

Coming out of Kristineberg T-bana station, take a right at Kristinebergskolan through the small park and walk past the school to the end of the street. Then turn left and take the small lane through the green space following it as it curves to the right. No, it's not the oak just before the underpass to the right; you'll have to continue on and take the underpass to finally reach the Birger Jarl Oak in front of the next bridge.

Address Böttigervägen, 11244 Stockholm-Kungsholmen | Public transport Kristineberg
(T-bana 17, 18, 19) | Tip The food in the Thai snack bar opposite the T-bana station
Kristineberg comes recommended. This is a good option for a little snack after a visit to
the venerable oak.

13___The Brunkeberg Tunnel

The ideal spot for an original photoshoot

It does feel a little like being in a science fiction movie. The walls of the tunnel tube – 231 metres (758 feet) long, four metres (13 feet) wide – are clad with bright-yellow slabs. The ceiling consists of corrugated iron and riveted metal illuminated by neon tubes at regular intervals. In photographs this somewhat futuristic effect is enhanced, accentuating even more the interesting shadow play between light and corrugated iron. At two points the cladding is broken, and a glimpse behind a wire netting reveals why the construction of the tunnel nearly turned into a fiasco in the late 19th century.

Old maps of Stockholm show a narrow ridge running across Norrmalm. Formed during the Ice Age, this ridge – made up of sand and debris – once divided the district. That goes some way towards explaining why the Brunkeberg Tunnel, which is reserved for pedestrians and cyclists, seems to be the only underground passage to have ever been drilled through what is known as the Brunkebergåsen.

This is where engineer Knut Lindmark, who made a name for himself with drawings for the old Katarinahissen lift, met his Waterloo. Loose rock debris on the western side caused the tunnel to collapse time and again. Only a freezer unit, originally invented for the transport of perishable goods by ship and rented especially from England, brought the solution the team longed for. The device allowed the scree to be cooled down to a temperature of minus 18 degrees, deep-freezing it as it were and allowing the crews to dig without interruption.

In 1886 King Oscar II inaugurated the tunnel, the passage of which initially cost two öre. The fee was abolished later, as the Stockholmers deemed it too expensive.

As the tunnel is secured on both sides by doors, it stays both pleasantly cool in summer and warm in winter. A spectacular setting for a futuristic photo shoot in any weather.

Address Between David Bagares gata 6 and Tunnelgatan 1a, 11137 Stockholm-Norrmalm | Public transport Hötorget (T-bana 17, 18, 19); David Bagares gata (bus 43) | Opening times 9am–10pm | Tip The flat of stuccoer Axel Notini can be visited at David Bagares gata 10. At the end of the 19th century he had the reputation as one of the masters of his profession. His residence, full of elaborate stucco work, is a good example of the living quarters of wealthy citizens at the time.

14__ Café Ekudden

Can there be a more idyllic place to fill up?

This is the place to laze about on the pier in relaxing large armchairs or sofas, watching the sunlight glitter on the Baltic Sea, elegant sailing yachts gliding past or fast motorboats being filled up at the turquoise-blue petrol pumps. The café on the pier serves various snacks and drinks, ensuring the visitors' well-being. You need to look closely for any indication that in the early 20th century there was a swimming pool here that was state-of-the-art for its time.

In fact, the inhabitants of Djursholm were already taking refreshing dips here in Aludden's bath house in the late 19th century. After the bath house fell victim to a storm in 1898, the Ekuddsbad was erected. The architect was Torben Grut no less, who had already built Stockholm's Olympic stadium. The pool became very popular, as people weren't allowed to swim everywhere at the time and the admission fee was low. One of the regulars was Wille Grut, who would go on to win gold for Sweden in modern pentathlon at the 1948 summer Olympics in London. It was at the Ekuddsbadet that he took his first tentative swims, apparently a bit grudgingly at first, and then only because his father had designed the pool.

As there was even a 20-metre/65-feet diving tower the place used to hold regular competitions. To prevent the tower from being torn away by a storm, it was fastened to the rock using iron hoops that can still be seen today. Another preserved part are some stone steps that used to lead into one of the pools.

During the 1940s, when Stockholm's lakes and waterways were suffering from heavy pollution, the baths were closed as a hazard to public health. 1961 saw the opening of the first café. Today, the place has two petrol pumps and as is the case with regular petrol stations one can purchase tools as well as provisions. This arguably is one of the most idyllic service areas around and has remained (for the time being at least) a bit of a secret.

Address Strandvägen 12, 18260 Stockholm-Djursholm | **Public transport** Danderyds Sjukhus (T-bana 13, 14),then continue to Djursholms torg with bus 601H, 606 | **Opening times** In summer Mon–Fri 11am–4pm, Sat and Sun 11am–5pm, longer in good weather | **Tip** Consider taking the Stormholmslinjen commuter boat here from Ropsten, a pleasant way to start off a summer day (www.lidingo.se).

15__The Car Park
Safe from nuclear fallout

In the 1950s, the Swedish government was occupied primarily with two major problems: fear of a nuclear attack and the lack of parking space due to the massive increase in private car ownership in the inner cities. Creating the Katarinaberget car park meant killing two birds with one stone: it can accommodate some 550 cars or 20,000 people.

In 1952 shafts were dynamited into the rock on both sides of Katarinaberget. While the two tunnels met eight months later, the building designed by architect Werner Allan was only completed in 1957. At the time, the complex was considered the world's largest nuclear shelter and Europe's largest car park. With a length of some 400 metres, it runs from Katarinavägen below Mosebacke torgs along Björngårdsgata.

Apart from a slightly eccentric poster near the Katarinavägen entrance, detailing the entire complex including its capacity levels, inside the car park little points to its use as a fallout shelter. Only the old-fashioned speakers dangling from the ceiling at short intervals seem a little unusual.

Yet just as any other of Stockholm's shelters Katarinaberget car park can be converted into a fully functional nuclear bunker within 48 hours.

In the case of war six gates, each weighing 51,400 kilos would be lowered, protecting the facility from the outside world. To this day, the technology remains fully functional. Emergency generators powered by seven diesel motors would provide the energy for (among others) a sophisticated ventilation system. The facility also includes a decontamination facility to eliminate radioactive fallout as well as an autonomous water supply system. During renovation work in 1980 the original 250 water closets were replaced by modern dry toilets.

OK KATARINABERGE

Rymmer 550 bilar
eller
20 000 personer

BETONGPORTAR

MASKINHUS

Mosebacke Torg

INFART TILL ÖVERSTA
GARAGEPLANET

MASKINHUS

Verkstad

Infart

Värt att veta om anläggningen

1952— 57 byggdes anläggningen
105 000 m³ berg har sprängts bort

Address Katarinavägen 16, 11645 Stockholm-Södermalm | **Public transport** Slussen (T-bana 13, 14, 17, 18, 19) | **Tip** At Mosebacke torg/corner of Svartensgatan a slightly bent air vent juts out of the lawn, hiding an entrance intended to serve as an additional access to the bunker.

750 000 volt-
ampere kan reservkraftverket producera
200 000 kg is rymmes i isbassängerna
20 000 pers. kan samtidigt skyddas i anläggn
5000 pers. kan beredas sovplatser i skyddsru
ca 550 bilar rymmes i garaget för parkering
102 000 liter bensin ryms i stationernas tan

16 Carl Eldh's Studio
At home with a sculptor

One of Sweden's most famous sculptors worked here for over three decades. Following his death in 1954 his wife and daughter left the studio of artist Carl Eldh as it was and opened it to the public. It offers a unique glimpse of a sculptor's work in the early 20th century. Even for those not that interested in statuary art and sculptures a visit of this light-filled house with its fascinating ambience will prove to be worthwhile.

The unusual wooden building occupies a remote position within the idyllic Bellevue park adjoining the lively Vasastan neighbourhood. Dating from 1919, the building was designed by architect Ragnar Östberg. It offered Carl Eldh the finest views of the Brunnsviken as well as the peace and quiet the sculptor needed for his work. The original idea had been for this superb building to serve also as a residence for the Eldh family. Unfortunately Östberg had forgotten to include any kind of insulation in his design, obliging the Eldhs to rent an additional flat.

The museum houses over 100 sculptures, busts and sketches as well as maquettes for famous works by the artist. Among the objects is a homeless mother with her child, visibly marked by hunger, and a woman lying on the floor is writhing in pain, mourning the loss of her baby.

Carl Eldh was interested in people and their fates; rank and status were of little interest to him. It was only in later years that he became known for portrait busts of various creative minds, including numerous representations of the poet August Strindberg. The two artists shared a close friendship, commemorated by a statue standing next to the studio.

Eldh would first prepare all his work in plaster of Paris before casting it in bronze. Inhaling the plaster dust caused an illness called silicosis, which he was to die from at the age of 80.

Address Lögebodavägen 10, 11347 Stockholm-Vasastan | Public transport Roslagstull
(bus 40, 70, 690, 691) | Opening times 25 May–31 Aug: Tue–Sun 11am–4pm;
Sept–27 Oct: Sat–Sun 11am–4pm | Tip Between May and October, the museum
offers various guided sculpture walks in the city (for more information see
www.eldhsatelje.se or ring tel. +468/6126560).

17 __ The Cedergren Tower

A construction period spanning 100 years

The red-brick tower juts out among the stately villas of Stocksund like a medieval castle. Whilst the "Cedergrenska tornet" was only completed in 1996, it is the oldest building in the area. In 1890 forest ranger Albert Gotthard Nestor Cedergren was the first to purchase a plot from the newly founded development company Stocksund AB.

Six years on, work started on the tower. Cedergren's original plan had been to erect a viewing tower at the highest point in the area; later he started dreaming about a fully-fledged tower house. However, it seems that he was more interested in the construction process than in its actual completion.

Cedergren commissioned craftsmen who set to work using time-consuming traditional techniques while he occupied himself with the surrounding park.

The completion of the project dragged on and over the years several architects were involved. Among them were well-known names such as Ferdinand Boberg, who designed the NK department store as well as Lars Israel Wahlmann, architect of Stockholm's Engelbrekts Kyrka church.

When Cedergren died in 1921 the building was not yet finished. In 1975 his last heir donated the tower and park to the forestry college. And when the Danderyd community eventually took it over in 1981, it had fallen rather derelict. However, as the tower had become a kind of icon for Stocksund, various sponsors were eventually found, allowing it to be finally completed in 1996, exactly 100 years after work had started.

The top floor of the five-storey building holds what is called the Knights' Hall. A set of steps leads up to a large roof terrace, offering fantastic views across Stockholm. The tower can be rented for seminars, weddings and other occasions.

Address Kungsvägen 2, 18279 Stockholm-Stocksund | Public transport Sjöstigen
(bus 601H) | Tip The park around the tower, with its tall pine, fir and cypress trees was
converted into a botanical garden by the Danderyd municipality, which opened it to the
public. A walk in the park is like a trip into another world.

18 — The China Mountain
A listed pile of shards

With its blindingly white walls Karlberg Palace occupies a grand position atop one arm of Lake Mälar opposite Kungsholmen. Serving as the summer residence of the royal family in the 17th century, the court moved here permanently after Tre Kronor castle was destroyed in a fire. Today, the well-kept complex houses the world's oldest military academy. From 1792 onwards Gustav III had officers trained here. The only slightly confusing presence is a hill rising on the edge of this venerable compound. Reminiscent of a dump heap, it is however surrounded by a neat green varnished fence. And not only that: this mound is actually listed. So what is there to protect here?

Nearly 300 years ago, a famous Swedish china manufacturer was located in the district. The Rörstrand company produced what was called feldspar china, very similar to fine bone china. Moreover, Rörstrand was also a leading manufacturer of tiled ovens. Shards of porcelain and rejects were thrown into the fenced-in dumping ground. When the company moved to Göteborg in 1926, the Stockholm operation was torn down, leaving only the mound of china detritus.

It's hard to imagine that there is much valuable china hiding between stones, grass and ground tendrils after all those years. Presumably a good number of people would have gone on a treasure hunt over the past decades, as the fence is not exactly insurmountably high. Lean far enough across it and you might discover the odd interesting shard. The piece over there with the green flower tendrils on a white background for instance could come from the well-known "Gröna Anna" china collection that Rörstrand produced between 1898 and 1943. Yet one needs to look closely to make it out between a variety of rubbish. These days glass shards from carelessly thrown-away beer bottles or a ceramics bowl with the inscription "Popcorn" are equally protected by the fence.

Address Karlbergs strand, 17173 Stockholm-Solna | Public transport Västra Skogen
(T-bana 10,11; bus 113, 196, 507) | Tip The 17th century palace park was originally laid
out in the French baroque style and converted into an English park in the 18th century, as
was the fashion at the time. A number of interesting buildings and monuments mean it's
well worth a stroll.

19_ The Church Library
A surprisingly secular place

Think of a church library and you'll be imagining interminable rows of Bible editions and other theological treatises filling the bookshelves. At the parish library of St Matthews' in Vasastan however, it's nothing strange to find the latest novels as well as pacy thrillers and books on natural history.

The library dates back to 1912, when many workers and clerks formed part of the congregation. A good share of them worked at the nearby Rörstrand porcelain factory. Municipal libraries would only come in towards the end of the 1920s, up to that point people's education was in the hands of the church libraries. So there were fairly strict rules in place at the St Matthew's parish library back in thoes days. In order to borrow a light-hearted novel one had to take out two other more worthy tomes as well.

Once Stockholm's big central library opened, most church libraries disappeared, which makes the St Matthew's library something of a rarity. Since 1916 it has been housed in the same rooms, designed specifically for this purpose when the house was originally built. The furnishings are all orginal: The fine cherry-wood shelves, the wood-panelled walls, the hardwood floor as well as the old-fashioned lamps all contribute to a cosy ambience. This is a deliberate move to counter the rush of today's hectic life. Another example of this approach is that the library's inventory is not managed by computer but with old-school index cards. Nor are all books arranged properly on the shelves; the occasional pile of books is still waiting to be sorted out. But that can wait. What is more important for the staff is to talk to and advise visitors. Which doesn't mean that one can't just browse in peace and quiet. There's a table with coffee and biscuits that visitors are welcome to enjoy against a small donation. And the sofa next to the table is just perfect for browsing.

Address Västmannagatan 92, 11343 Stockholm-Vasastan | Public transport Odenplan
(T-bana 17, 18, 19); Norrtullsgatan (bus 2, 40) | Opening times Mon–Tue 2–7pm,
Wed 10am–3pm, Thu 2–7pm, Fri 10am–1pm | Tip At house number 79 in the same
street, the "Slatgo & Clemenza" shop sells interesting hats by the "New York Hat & Cap
Co." brand as well as vintage-style bags, ties and cufflinks (Wed–Sat 12 noon–6pm,
Sat 12 noon–4pm).

20__ The Cinema City

A stroll through the history of film

The cast-iron entrance gate with its neon red letters still offers a glimpse of the high life that once prevailed here. When it was inaugurated in 1920, "Filmstaden" was one of the biggest and most modern studios of its time. By today's standards it seems rather small, which might also be down to the fact that only eight of the neoclassical buildings have been preserved. They house artists' studios, restaurants and offices.

However, grabbing an audioguide and taking a stroll through the area, the hustle and bustle of that era comes to life again. One can imagine how sensational the studio was with its glass roof. How wardrobe girls, screenwriters, directors, script girls and technicians were scurrying around awaiting the stars that were chauffeured in by limousines. How a certain Greta Lovisa Gustafsson played her first film role here in 1924 which was to take her on to Hollywood shortly after as Greta Garbo.

Legendary parties were held in the former canteen which today houses a restaurant.

No-one got preferential treatment in this simple white-panelled room, stars had to queue like anybody else. Only director Ingmar Bergman, whose name (always mentioned with awe) keeps cropping up during the tour, enjoyed special privileges.

The history of Filmstaden is also a lesson in the history of the 20th-century film industry: from the golden years of the silent films in the 1920s and the beginnings of the talkies in the 1930s all the way to the Nouvelle Vague that spilled over from France.

A desire for more authenticity however soon had the directors turn towards original locations, in the end rendering the studios obsolete.

By the 1960s, other cultural institutions had moved into a part of the buildings until the last wrap was called in 1969.

Address Greta Garbos väg 3, 16940 Stockholm-Solna, www.filmstadenskultur.se | Public transport Näckrosen (T-bana 11; bus 156, 176, 177, 302, 515, 595) | Opening times Fri–Sun 11am–6pm; the audioguide is available from Café "Portvaktsstugan". The homepage also lists guided tours. | Tip Café "Portvaktsstugan" in the former porter's office at the entrance is a good place to nibble good waffles and to find out more about Swedish film history and its stars.

21 __ The Citykyrkan
A place for singing and dancing

At a time when many churches are deconsecrated and converted into event locations, things have gone the opposite way with the Citykyrkan. The initials FP in the glass pane of the entrance door still point to the fact that this place used to be the swanky Fenix Palace. The building was the work of architect Hjalmar Westerlund who created an elegant concert hall with a bar and restaurant area.

In 1912 the Felix Palace opened its doors for the first time. During the first few years the singer and actor Ernst Rolf ensured a full house with his revue performances.

When business suffered under prohibition in 1919, the palace changed hands, and the Fenix Palace was converted into a live music restaurant, staging shows with both national and international artists. Twice a week public dance events were held. In the 1930s, big-name Swedish jazz musicians would appear here. With the outbreak of World War II however, the establishment hit rocky ground and had to close down.

In 1940 the Pentecostal congregation took over the building, which it still owns. The church had a baptismal font built into the orchestra pit in the back part of the stage, but otherwise changed little about the furnishings. The balconies with their ornate gold decorations, the huge crystal chandeliers and the impressive glass ceiling may be visited to this day. The opulent foyer houses the former ticket booth, its pane still bearing the phoenix bird, the former symbol of the dance hall.

Sunday services in the Citykyrkan make the spirit of the Fenix Palace come alive again. The congregation singing at the top of their lungs create a superb atmosphere. Rousing gospel concerts are regularly held. It might even happen that the cantor performs a somersault jump over the baptismal font and at the end of the service half the congregation join in swinging on stage.

Address Adolf Fredriks kyrkogata 10, 11137 Stockholm-Norrmalm, www.cks.se | Public transport Hötorget (T-bana 17, 18, 19); Adolf Fredriks kyrka (bus 59) | Opening times Information on religious services and events can be found on the homepage | Tip The first floor of the same building houses the impressively designed "City Konditori". Indulge in delicious tarts in a sophisticated ambience under chandeliers (Mon–Fri 10am–6pm, Sat 10am–2pm).

22_ The Dancefloor
For incurable romantics

If you suddenly hear swing music piping up amidst the greenery while taking a stroll through the extensive park area of Stora Skuggan then chances are you're close to one of the city's most romantic locations: "Stora Skuggans Dansbana".

The open pavilion lies on a small pond surrounded by shrubs and trees.

Wooden planks make up the dance floor. The railing is surrounded by narrow benches for the dancers to recover whilst enjoying idyllic views over the water. The wooden roof is painted white, lending the place a certain Dixie flair redolent of the American South.

Fittingly, on summer Sundays, this is a regular meeting point for "Lindy Hop" aficionados. Emerging during the first half of the past century, this type of swing dance was the first to include acrobatic elements. While the sun is reflected on the water in front of the pavilion and the ducks make their calm rounds, the dancers swirl across the dance floor swinging their hips. Everybody is welcome to join in the dance or to just watch and listen to the music.

The Stora Skuggan Dansbana is also popular with fans of the "Square Dance", a folk dance originally from the US. These events usually have slightly older dancers following the instructions of a compere, dancing together in a circle, turning left and right or spinning around with a partner.

The dance floor events came up towards the end of the 19th century and early 20th century and had their heyday in the 1930s and 1940s. Many sports clubs set up covered outdoor spaces welcoming a mainly young audience dancing to contemporary jazz music.

With the advent of discos in the 1970s however, the dance floors disappeared. But a few remain, letting the old times roll again.

Address Stora Skuggans väg, 11542 Stockholm-Norra Djurgården, www.facebook.com/
StoraSkuggan | Public transport Universitetet (T-bana 13, 14); Stora Skuggan (bus 40) |
Opening times In summer Sun 4pm–8pm; more information online | Tip Also located
in Stora Skuggan, the "4h-gård" farm is open to the public daily between 10am and 3pm.
Small children can go pony-riding and bigger ones take part in a proper hack. Coffee and
cake is served too.

3 The Danviks Cliff

Urban climbing

Passing Danviks Bridge in the direction of Nacka and looking to the right reveals a steep rock wall right in the heart of the city. The cliff is very popular in rock-climbing circles so it's fascinating to stop for a while and watch. Scores of bouldering aficionados looking for particular challenges come here to practise.

The wall is full of sharp edges that require special leg work. There's no time to get bored here as climbers can choose between 14 different ascents.

Admittedly, it's a slightly bizarre sight. Standing above the crag on a kind of plateau, the colourful residential high-rises of Danviksklippan neighbourhood are commonly known as pencil houses for their pointed roofs.

Alongside the steep wall traffic roars across Dankviks Bridge, connecting Södermalm and Södra Hammarbyhamnen, and below the crag ships pass through the narrow canal.

The rock wall owes its particular texture to the fact that is was created by an artificial blasting operation rather than by the forces of nature. In the early 20th century, the lock between the Baltic Sea and Lake Mälar was no longer able to deal with the steadily increasing maritime traffic and the search was on for an alternative connection between the two bodies of water.

Construction of the Hammarbyleden, an artificial waterway running through Liljeholmviken and Årstaviken and flowing into the Baltic Sea at the Danviks Canal lasted from 1918 to 1925. As part of the work, the bays of Skanstull and Danvikstull were broadened by blasting.

The best way to watch climbers on Danviks cliff is to find a spot on a bench on the opposite bank. From there one can follow spellbound as the fit athletes, secured by ropes, work their way up the steep wall in no time at all.

Address Danviksklippan, 11644 Stockholm-Södermalm | Public transport Henriksdal (commuter train); Danviksklippan (bus 53) | Tip In summer, the "Boule & Berså" bar on the other side of the bridge provides the opportunity to play a round of boule or to just enjoy a cool drink in a relaxing ambience looking out onto the water. The only thing to remember is that it's cash only here.

24 Dessert & Choklad
Unbridled indulgence

Incredible, this kanelbullar cinnamon roll. So moist, cinnamonny and sweet, yet not overly so. Just right. And don't get us started on the blueberry roll. The intensive aroma of the fruits combines with the chewy dough to a unique tasting experience. Conrad Tyrsén and Ted Johansson rightly display the pastries and chocolates they make at their patisserie here as you would gems: in small drawers and display cases. The trained chefs quickly found out that their true passion lies in desserts. This is where they're able to make the most of their creativity.

Their motto being quality, the gourmet bakers only use the best ingredients. Just like Conrad the raspberries for the chocolates and pastries are from Gotland, and Ted buys the aromatic strawberries from his home region in southern Sweden. The figs are brought in from France. No matter whether it's little tarts, aromatic sourdough bread, fresh croissants, bullars, juicy semlors, compositions from chocolate and fruit or fine bonbons, the owners and their ten staff treat all products with the same care and love. What's more, they live the way they work: as dedicated gourmets.

Yet "Dessert & Choklad" is no elitist gastronomic sanctuary that caters only to wealthy Stockholmers. The ambience in the small shop is warm and prices absolutely affordable. People always have time for a little chat here. And not only that: when a neighbour and faithful customer expressed the wish to learn baking she was immediately invited to come and see how the delicacies were made in the bakery.

Regular customers of the friendly bakery include not only neighbourhood residents, but also the city hall. In 2012 "Dessert & Choklad" supplied the dessert for the gala dinner at the Nobel Prize award ceremony: a trilogy of cherries and mascarpone in a pistachio casing. The same delight, slightly modified, is now for sale at the shop. Ted and Conrad also designed and baked the wedding cake for Princess Victoria and her Daniel.

Address Patentgatan 7, 11267 Stockholm-Lilla Essingen | **Public transport** Luxparken (bus 49) | **Opening times** Tue–Fri 9–6pm, Sat and Sun 9am–4pm | **Tip** At Primusgatan 116, a red-brick former factory building houses a fine restaurant: "Lux" serves excellent food, at a price.

25 — The Diesel Works

How the first person reached the South Pole

Today, the old brick building that used to house a diesel factory in the Nacka district is a modern arts centre with café, cinema, theatre and concert hall. In the light-filled space nothing points to what lies hidden 20 metres/65 feet below: an archaic world in its own right. The only way to enter the labyrinthine corridors of the former industrial facility, its rock walls adorned with large-scale photographs portraying its history, is with a guide. The factory was founded in 1898, after Oscar Lamm and Marcus Wallenberg had bought the design of a motor off the German engineer Rudolf Diesel, without knowing whether it would actually function. Once initial problems were overcome the diesel motor eventually developed into a true rival for the steam engine. When in 1911 the Norwegian polar explorer Roald Amundsen became the first person to reach the South Pole, it was aboard a diesel-powered ship – a revolution. He reached his goal a month before his British rival Scott and unlike Scott was to return alive.

In 1951 the production of diesel motors was relocated. Instead, from 1956 on compressed air machines were manufactured in Nacka and employed world-wide in tunnel construction.

Together with the pictures on the wall, the special ambience in these rock vaults conveys a lively impression of the former bustling activities, an impression amplified by the fact that a neighbouring pit is still used for trial blasts. During the visit you might well hear detonations. No wonder many former employees lost their hearing. Work was hard and accidents a frequent occurrence. Which makes it all the more surprising that in the 1950s the first women went down into the pit. In many countries women were not allowed to work underground; not so in Sweden. The only conundrum that posed itself was the dress issue: were women to wear skirts underground?

Address Marcusplatsen 17, 13134 Nacka | **Public transport** Nacka Sickla (commuter train, bus 401, 403, 469, 491) | **Tip** The nearby "Le Fou" circus school at Exprimentvägen 7 offers classes for children from five or six years, up to adult age. Minimum age 15 for those dropping in without notice (www.circuslefou.se).

26 — Djupforsen

A playground for children from two to 102

Beep, beep, it sounds from the left. Beeep. Beeep. Beaming with pleasure, a little girl in a prop airliner keeps sounding the horn. Beep. Beep. Various children's legs are dangling out of the belly of a rocket, and on the other side a little boy whizzes down a slide shouting with joy. In the library a story is read followed by a handful of intently listening children. A little boy is looking for the way out of a maze while in front a girl is touching the sky on a swing.

This is Djupforsen, the home of Mulle Meck, better known in English-speaking countries as Gary Gadget. The creation of Swedish children's authors George Johansson and Jens Ahlbom is a mechanic who knows how to turn anything into something. For him there is no such thing as junk, only things that haven't found their destination yet. His favourite pastime is building means of transport, and here in Djupforsen you will be able to admire a few unusual specimens.

Designed by set designer Tor Svae, the imaginative playground was launched in 2008. At the entrance visitors are welcomed by Gary and his dog Buffa. Many friends of Gary's live here too: the artist Gårdån van Gågg, whose favourite subject are crying elks at sundown. Gabriella Gourmet and Gaston Garcon, who run the restaurant "Chez Vous", and Daisy Diesel, who is able to do nearly anything and will help anybody.

Visitors are informed where the residents come from, what they like to eat and which hidden talents they harbour. The latter range from skateboarding and playing the balalaika to "simply being friendly".

The weather forecast in Djupforsen is the responsibility of a little fir cone: if it's moist, it's raining. If it casts a shadow, the sun is shining. If it has a white top, there is snow, and if you can't see the cone, it's foggy. It's as simple as that.

Address Mönstringsvägen 9, 17069 Stockholm-Solna | Public transport Ulriksdal, plus 10 minutes' walk (commuter train no. 36); Fridensborgsvägen (bus 540) | Opening times Daily, all year round | Tip Opposite the entrance to Djupforsen you will find a basketball pitch for older children.

27 __ The Djursholm Beach

Springboard into the Baltic Sea

Djursholm is one of the wealthiest municipalities in Sweden. Many of the stately villas here date back to the turn of the 20th century, and lying as they do amidst park-like surroundings, they seem more like palaces. During the week a near-eerie silence reigns here. In the front gardens lonely trampolines and high-octane barbecue sets, abandoned bobby cars and tricycles wait for the return of their owners from school, kindergarden, work or from their summer house in Schärengarten.

This is where you'll find Skärsnäsväg, a quiet residential street. On fine summer days however, it can at times turn into a busy thoroughfare. In the early morning or at weekends people clad in bathrobes scurry past, some of them driving big SUVs, others on a bike or hurrying by on foot. None of their own swimming pools offer what they find here. And only local residents know about it.

A bumpy footpath leads across the meadow opposite house number 3 in the direction of the sea, eventually turning right, towards a barbecue area. Turning left there and crossing another short stretch of meadow brings you to the secret spot: jutting out a good six feet into the sea from a small concrete ledge is a springboard overlooking the Baltic Sea. It's not actually that important which style you prefer, cannon ball, header, or simply holding your nose: this jump into the Baltic Sea, bouncing up and down and diving in, is an incomparable experience. Whether climbing up the ladder again straight away and diving in once more or enjoying a little swim first is up to personal preference.

For the weekend rush hour there might be five people thronging the place at the same time, but during the week swimmers are often on their own. Sunbathing on the rocks, taking a high jump into the cool water again and again and firing up the grill for a barbecue … who needs a villa when you've got this?

Address Skärsnäsvägen, 18263 Stockholm-Djursholm | Public transport Djursholms torg (bus 606) | Tip There is a small sandy beach suitable for small children close by. Instead of following the path towards the water to the end, simply cross the lawn to your right.

28 Ernst Herman Thörnberg

The Socrates of Stockholm

It is quite easy to overlook him. And most of those who do spot him don't know the identity of this little bronze man who has been standing outside the eastern entrance to the Brunkeberg Tunnel since 1987.

In the 1950s, when Norrmalm was still called Klara and life in the narrow alleyways was determined by tin and type foundries, stamp sellers, basket makers, groceries and pet shops instead of today's shopping arcades and chain stores, you would have seen this man pass by the Brunkeberg Tunnel each day. What caught the eye was the way he dressed. He would always wear a fur hat as well as two jackets or coats. The shoes were stuck inside galoshes and his ears stuffed with cotton balls.

This slightly eccentric exterior hid one of the country's most erudite personalities. Ernst Herman Thörnberg (1873–1961), also called the "Socrates of Klara" by the neighbourhood residents, was a merchant by training but worked as a journalist, researching Swedish migratory movements on several trips through Europe and the USA. Eventually he gained such a wealth of knowledge of social sciences that the Reichstag provided him with grants for his research. In 1939 the University of Uppsala awarded him an honorary PhD in philosophy. In Stockholm he would spend his days in the Royal Library to expand his already enormous knowledge base and to pass it on to others in lectures.

This bronze sculpture by Swedish artist Ulf Didrik Sucksdorff serves as a monument to the eccentric philosopher, who actually owed his extravagant dress style to various phobias. Thörnberg was terrified of thunderstorms, appreciating galoshes most of all for their capacity to act as lightning rods. The great man also lived in fear of bacteria and hated noise. Hence the cotton balls, which, looking closely, you will spot on the sculpture too.

Address Tunnelgatan, 11137 Stockholm-Norrmalm | Public transport Hötorget (T-bana 17, 18, 19); David Bagares gata (bus 43) | Tip At Johannesgatan 16, the Drottninghus (built in 1686) goes back to an initiative of queen Ulrika Eleonora. From 1733 it was a residential home for "poor, ill or needy widows and daughters of officers, civil servants, clerics, citizens or court officials"; today, it is a care home for the elderly.

29 The Five Trumpet Blasts
A touch of New York

It's easy to just walk by or dismiss them as an eyesore of the past century. Viewed from the south-eastern corner of the Sergels torg square (Hamngatan, corner of Sergelarkaden), the five high-rises form a staggered architectural ensemble that is a little reminiscent of Manhattan. Reaching 72 metres/236 feet, the skyscrapers – each with 19 floors – are an example of the functionalist zeitgeist whose roots go back to the Sweden of the 1930s and which remained en vogue up into the 1960s. Functional equalled beautiful. This aesthetics was accompanied by a strong belief in the future. Which is why at the high-rises' inauguration in 1966, mayor Yngve Larsson compared them euphorically to five trumpet blasts welcoming a new era.

Back in the 1930s the old Klara neighbourhood was supposed to be torn down and replaced with a kind of downscaled New York, featuring skyscrapers in the art deco style. Famous architects including Le Corbusier submitted draft suggestions on how to redesign the neighbourhood. However, the war caused the project to be delayed. Once the redevelopment of the city centre was finally decided in 1944, architect David Helldén was commissioned to draw up plans for the design. He allegedly insisted on five houses as this was the number of roses always given to a woman.

The skyscrapers were designed by prestigious Swedish architecture firms who – following the American example – chose the curtain wall system. The original plans had the windowless front side flashing neon advertising, thus transforming Sergels torg into a diminutive Times Square.

In the 1970s the general cultural climate had changed and criticism of the city's rigorous demolition policy became more vociferous. After all, redevelopment had claimed 750 buildings, including some of great cultural and historical value.

Address Sergels torg, 11157 Stockholm-Norrmalm | Public transport T-Centralen
(T-bana 10, 11, 13, 14, 17, 18, 19) | Tip With a length of 1.5 kilometres/nearly a mile and
inaugurated in 1911, the Kungsgatan came to be regarded as Stockholm's Broadway in the
1930s and 1940s. While it initially lost out to the new Sergels torg, following refurbishment
in the 1990s the boulevard is now resplendent again.

30__Folckers Snörmarkeri
Pompoms, tassels, ribbons …

From the outside the only conspicious item is a pretty antique rocking horse in the window. The various baskets outside are filled with ribbons. A crafts' shop? Sowing supplies? Not really. Folckers sell tassels, bobbles, pompoms, as well as borders, ribbons and braids. That and only that, but in all variations imaginable.

The small shop is a world all its own. Shiny silk tufts dangle from the ceiling, pompoms in all colours of the rainbow spill out of a basket over there and bobbles with rhinestone trimmings are suspended from a rack.

Somehow you expect a man in knickerbockers and silk stockings or a lady in a crinoline dress to step into the shop any minute. Instead, an elderly gentleman shuffles in and pushes a worn-down tasselled border with pompoms across the counter. It takes the shop assistant thirty seconds to pull an identical model from the drawer. Identical, yet brand new. The old gentleman is beaming.

In 1890 the Hein family founded a company specialising in textile furnishings, moving into the Hornsgatan in 1936. Most tassels are custom-made for Folckers in traditional workshops in Belgium, Germany and Italy, some models however come out of their own studio.

The shop stocks centenary tassels, as well as a large selection of trims for furniture from the various decades of the past century. Also for sale are lamps and silk-covered electric cables – in any colour of course.

Since 2003 John Johansson and Tino Rivero have continued to run the family business with great commitment. Their customers include fashion houses, set designers, theatres and the royal court. However, when a young man with dreadlocks enters the shop to ask for needle and thread, John Johansson can't oblige. With a friendly smile he recommends a shop in the neighbourhood.

Address Hornsgatan 52, 11821 Stockholm-Södermalm | Public transport Mariatorget (T-bana 13, 148) | Tip "Judits Secondhand" at Hornsgatan 75 stocks selected vintage clothing from the 1950s and 1970s. And at Hornsgatan 65 "Herr Judit" offers vintage clothing for men.

31_ The Forest Spring

A special nature experience

This image would come as much less of a surprise were you to come across it on a mountain hike or somewhere in the countryside: fresh, cool, crystal-clear water flowing out of a slope. However, this spring is located in a wooded area only a fifteen-minute bus ride from Stockholm's city centre.

In other places large signposts would presumably point the way to the spring. The water would be credited with curative powers and sold for a lot of money in pretty purpose-designed bottles.

Not so in Stockholm's Nacka neighbourhood. Here the spring bubbles peacefully and undisturbed out of two provisionally installed pipes below an old tree whose gnarly roots cover the ground.

Next to it is a photograph of a man with Native American features leaning against a trunk and forming the centre of a makeshift altar. Native Americans revere and respect nature. Maybe whoever set up that small installation wanted to remind visitors of this.

Here nobody makes a quick buck from the spring. Only small, easily missed signs point the way for those determined to find it. The best starting points are the Tenntorp bus stop or the gardening accessories shop across the road, "JH:s Blom & Trädgård".

From there follow the road a little in the direction of Äventyrsbana, a climbing garden.

Where the forest starts, small wooden signs pointing to "Källa" initially lead on to a broad path. However, the closer the goal, the sparser the signage. The last marker sends nature lovers off the main path right into the trees. Shortly thereafter the dirt track forks.

Take the right-hand path. After about 200 metres, just when the feeling sets in that one has walked too far, the sound of murmuring water can be heard.

Address Velamsund Nature Reserve, Älvtavägen, 13133 Stockholm-Nacka | Public transport
Tenntorp (bus 401, 491, 821) | Tip The "JH:s Blom & Trädgård" shop at Älvtavägen 107 sells
home-made jams and juices.

32 __ The Fox

It even happened to the clever fox

Shrouded in blankets, he sits in front of the Riksgatan that leads to Gamla stan. His eyes look sad and a little befuddled, as if he can't quite understand how he ended up there.

The "Hemlös Räv", or homeless fox, is a bronze sculpture by British artist Laura Ford. It forms part of the "Rag and Bone" series inspired by characters imagined by the English children's author Beatrix Potter.

In 2008 the city of Stockholm purchased the fox, who serves as a reminder of those living without a roof over their heads. Readers of the homeless newspaper "Situation" voted on where the fox was supposed to end up. Placing him here, right opposite Stockholm's Reichstag was presumably intended as a statement to remind politicians not to forget the poor and the homeless.

Of the just under 800,000 Stockholmians some 3000 live on the street, with the number of homeless children in particular increasing. This is where Stockholm's "Stadsmission" comes in. The independent organisation seeks to alleviate the abject poverty of homeless people in the short term and to work towards improving their situation in the long term. The organisation funds itself through monetary and material donations as well as subsidies from the government. Moreover, the Stadsmission runs cafés, bakeries and various second-hand shops. These sell clothing, books, crockery, lamps and jewellery and actually enjoy a very hip reputation. The Stadsmission even has its own fashion label: "Remake" brings together furniture, clothing and accessories from recycled materials designed by both famous names and design students.

Those who feel inspired to do good by seeing the fox can check the Stadsmission homepage for information on what's currently needed and make a contribution. This can be something as simple as some soap, toothbrushes or toothpaste.

Address Drottninggatan/corner with Strömgatan, 11151 Stockholm-Norrmalm, www.stadsmissionen.se | Public transport Kungsträdgården (T-bana 10, 11) | Tip The Stadsmission café on Stortorget 3 in Gamla stan not only serves fine cake, it also sells delicious bread from the in-house bakery. And all in aid of a good cause!

33__ The Fredhällsbad
Urban swimming

When the sun burns down relentlessly, clothes stick to the skin and the craving for a refreshing jump into cold water becomes too intense, this turns into one of the most attractive spots in Stockholm. The nearby Traneberg Bridge with its impressive concrete construction lends an urban flair to a dip in Lake Mälaren. After the swim, rocks and a small lawn provide ample opportunity for sunbathing and chilling. Painted in bright candy colours and lovingly furnished, the café there serves cool drinks and throws in a little arts exhibition as well. A few elderly ladies chat outside the green-and-white bathhouse. Occasionally one of them will descend a ladder and gently slide into the water.

Fredhällsbadet was one of Stockholm's first public baths. In 1916 a huge complex with hotel and restaurant was planned for this location. What is there today was only intended to be the beginning but the rest was never realised.

In 1922 the facility was inaugurated with the Nordic Swimming Competition and named Traneberg Baths. At the time there were not only separate bath houses for men and women, a tall board fence ensured virtue and order were maintained between the sexes. Whilst the fence has gone, the separate bath houses are still in use. When in 1946 the original plans were dug out and the baths about to be pulled down, the "Fredhäll Baths Club" took over operations and managed to save it. In the summer months anyone can swim here for free. In the winter months this is a privilege reserved for club members.

Those who like it quieter can just walk past the Fredshällsbadet and follow the street to the end where a dirt track carries on into the rocks. Even in summer there is always a little spot here offering privacy. There is one caveat however: a bit of physical fitness is required to get into the water from here and, more importantly, out again.

Address Snoilskyvägen 34, 11254 Stockholm-Kungsholmen | Public transport Kristineberg (T-bana 17, 18, 19); Frödingsvägen (bus 49, 62) | Opening times June–Aug daily 9am–7pm | Tip The restaurant "Solstugan" at Snoilskyvägen 37 serves simple dishes on several terrace levels, but it's also possible to merely enjoy a drink with views over the glittering waters of Lake Mälaren (Mon–Sat 10.30am–11pm, Sun 10.30am–10pm).

34__From Ropsten to Lappis

A little countryside trip in the city

This walk, under five kilometres/3 miles, is for those who would like to grab a slice of countryside within the city-centre. In early summer the rape fields are in blossom, whilst in autumn the forest displays its colourful leaves to best advantage. Those longing for solitude will enjoy this walk too.

The starting point is the T-bana station Ropsten, exit Hjortha-gen. From there, sports grounds and a path leading past them on the left-hand side can be identified. Follow this path, which will eventually pass an abandoned gas works. The impressive red-brick gasometers were designed at the end of the 19th century by the well-known Swedish architect Ferdinand Boberg. The works were closed down in 2011 and will probably be converted into residential space.

Beyond the gas works' grounds the path leads on to Boberggatan, where you immediately turn right into Norra Fiskartorpsvägen. Shortly after take a right at the pedestrian crossing and immediately after that a left into the forest. After passing a small wooden bridge, turn right into Fiskartorpsvägen. A rural pastoral landscape, not much changed since the Iron Age, now stretches out on the left. Sheep, cows and highland cattle graze in the lush green setting. Take a left into Husarviksvägen and past "Ropstens Båtklubb". On the other side of the water the villas of Lidingö come into view.

At this point just follow the street, which has very little traffic, and turn right towards Ugglebo into Lilla Skuggas väg. Keeping left in the direction of the forest and following the forest track always parallel to the water, you'll emerge at the Lappis students' hall of residence. The small bay here has a sandy beach. During term-time this spot is used for many wild parties to the beat of loud music. When the students are on holiday though, you'll have the bathing spot practically to yourself.

Address T-bana Station Ropsten, 11543 Stockholm-Hjorthagen | Public transport Start: Ropsten (T-bana 13), or end point: Universitetet (T-bana 13, 14) | Tip Lots of blueberries can be picked on the way by those who opt for the stroll in August.

35 _ The Friday Lecture

Interesting events open to anybody

The "Konstfack" is Sweden's largest art and design college. Founded as far back as 1844, it is in fact anything but traditional. When the university moved into the former Ericsson telephone factory in 2004, the 1930s structure was transformed into a state-of-the-art building that is filled with light. Today, exhibition galleries for students' work have joined lecture halls, workshops and computer workstations across more than 20,000 square metres. The bright "Vita Havet" atrium also serves as an exhibition space, changing its appearance with every project.

An international and very open atmosphere reigns here, as the Konstfack is partnered with over 50 universities from more than 25 countries.

Every year some 70 foreign students come here to study, while Stockholm students take an exchange semester at a partner university. So it's not surprising that lectures and the basic curriculum are predominantly taught in English.

The curriculum comprises the so-called "Friday's Lecture", a public event that specifically welcomes guests: each semester, university chancellor Maria Lantz and journalist Susanne Helgeson invite artists and professors from all over the world to deliver an interesting and unusual presentation.

When the subject was "Reality and Fiction – The Concious and the Unconscious" for instance, a brain researcher presented his work on unconscious learning, questioning all traditional theories of learning.

In the same cycle, one artist presented a mix of lecture and performance with music, images and texts. No matter the form or the subject – a Friday's Lecture is always an avantgarde event that inspires listeners and sends them on their way with new food for thought.

Address LM Ericssons väg 14, 12637 Stockholm-Hägersten, www.konstfack.se | **Public transport** Telefonplan (T-bana 14; bus 141, 142, 161, 190) | **Opening times** During term time: Fri 2–4pm, see the homepage for a list of lectures | **Tip** The Konstfack boasts one of the biggest art and design libraries in Sweden. Apart from books, samples of all sorts of materials can be borrowed. There is also an extensive art video collection.

36_ The Gallows Hill

An execution place amidst a residential area

Rising from the modest multi-family houses of the Hammarby-höjden residential neighbourhood is a rocky hill topped by a few trees. Today, the little hill looks innocuous and offers fine views of Stockholm. In the 17th and 18th centuries however this was a place of terror: Stockholm's gallows' hill, the city's execution site.

In the 15th and 16th centuries, the gallows stood on the Stigberg on Södermalm island, before being transferred to the hill south of Skanstull when Stockholm expanded. The gallows consisted of a round sturdy brick substructure upon which three tall stone pillars stood. Heavy beams were affixed between them to hang the condemned from.

The executions had up to ten people killed at the same time and were held in public – the idea was to encourage those watching to keep on the straight and narrow. In another effort to deter would-be offenders the cadavers were left to dangle for days. On their way to the gallows the condemned would pass the Götgatan and be served their last schnaps in the "Hamburger Keller" tavern, which at the time stood at the corner with Folkungagatan.

Some famous personalities were amongst those strung up at Hammarbyhöjden. One of them was Jacob Johan Anckarström, executed here in 1792 after assassinating King Gustav III at a masqued ball with a shot in the back.

After the executions the dead were buried in a pit next to the gallows. It is said that during construction of the Hammarbyhöjden neighbourhood in the 1930s workers found various bones. At the time they were asked to keep quiet to avoid scaring away future tenants.

Nowadays history is dealt with openly: a memorial was erected at the foot of the hill in Solandergatan and stones mark the place where the gallows used to stand.

Address Solandergatan, 12145 Stockholm-Hammarbyhöjden | Public transport Skärmarbrink (T-bana 17); Solandergatan (bus 193, 194) | Tip In a small park next to Hammarbyhöjden underground station, a bronze sculpture commemorates Willy Brandt, the German Social-Democrat politician who lived in Stockholm between 1940 and 1945 after fleeing Nazi Germany.

37__The Garden on Rails
Not your usual allotment association

Thinking of a Stockholm allotment association probably brings to mind a clutch of pretty little colourful wooden houses amidst picturesque gardens, wooden fences marking the exact borders between individual plots. Between spring and autumn a lot of digging goes on with the objective of harvesting fruit and vegetables from your own garden. However, those who apply for such a gem in adult age might have to wait until they are pensioners before they receive a plot.

But there is an alternative, offered by the "Trädgård på Spåret" or Garden on Rails association. On former railway grounds between Årstaviken and the Ringvägen large wooden crates stand next to rusty railway tracks, the alternative plots of this unusual allotment association. Filled to the brim with soil, these boxes are used by the association's members to grow vegetables.

The initiative was launched by Philipp Olsmeyer, a German living in Stockholm. The idea came to Olsmeyer in 2011 when he discovered the unused area in the heart of Södermalm island. Inspired by an alternative horticultural project in Berlin and in collaboration with German architect Max Zinnecker, Olsmeyer talked Stockholm's authorities into renting the unused area out to them. In no time they had gathered fellow horticultural activists to found an association, as well as sponsors to provide wooden crates, soil, seeds and gardening tools. In the autumn of 2012 the proud allotment gardeners were able to harvest their first box-grown vegetables.

Today, the association has 300 members, 30 of whom regularly work the soil here. It's not only the satisfying experience of eating radishes and courgettes from their own patch they enjoy, for many it's also the gardening work itself and the exchange of ideas within the community. There is even a café now, opening on summer weekends. The allotment gardeners sell coffee and home-made cake out of a colourfully painted construction trailer. Visitors are most welcome.

Address Below the Clarion Hotel on Ringvägen, 11860 Stockholm-Södermalm | Public transport Skanstull (T-bana 17, 18, 19; or bus 3, 4, 55, 74, 94, 96, 164, 193–195, 791, 794) | Tip At Ringvägen 94 a large mosaic with the symbol of the BP petroleum company can be seen. Part of a former petrol station inaugurated in 1954 the mosaic consists of 50,000 glass mosaic tiles in green, yellow and black and is considered to be Sweden's most beautiful advertising hoarding.

38_ The G. H. Herrsalong

For gentlemen with style

At first glance, the charm of the 1970s furnishings in muted shades of green wouldn't suggest that this gem has already been around for 150 years. However, this is a shop with a long tradition, providing real gentlemen with real quality.

"We do anybody's and everybody's hair and beards" says Günter Hansel, dressed in a knee-length white coat and black trousers, happy to chat. Originally from Germany, he has been living in Stockholm since 1971 and up until 2009 was running the salon together with his colleague Kurt Gerber – hence the G. H. initials of the firm's name. When Christer Åhnberg took over the salon, Hansel went into semi-retirement, only coming in on Mondays. However, the brass sign bearing his name remains on its accustomed spot on any day. Next to it are orderly rows of English quality products that no other salon in the city stocks.

For eight years, Günter Hansel cut the King's hair. On those occasions he would always have to go to the palace. It was Günter who coiffed Carl Gustaf for his wedding with Sylvia as well as for his first stamp. The customer is king here – in the true sense of the word but also in the figurative sense. For instance there was a man who asked Günter Hansel to simply comb his hair, every day, for years. Generally, the G.H. Herrsalong's has a mixed clientele, but due to its location, many bankers, lawyers and brokers frequent it.

Completely at ease, the two men stand at the shop window, their arms loosely folded in front of them, nodding time and again at people passing by. The younger generation likes to come in here too, as they can get the proper wet shave with a razor. That's a skill no longer taught these days. Moreover, Christer and Günter still maintain the art of a proper haircut in the classic style so that the hair simply keeps its shape. It is all about the classic men's cut that is apparently coming back into fashion, as the two reveal. "Out of bed" is so noughties now …

Address Lästmakargatan 6, 11144 Stockholm-Norrmalm | Public transport Östermalmstorg (T-bana 13, 14); Norrlandsgatan (bus 1, 56, 291) | Tip "Café & Cycles" at Norrlandsgatan 20 sells bikes made by the Italian cult brand Bianchi and the café next door serves fine Italian espresso.

39 __ The Grand Hotel
Second table from the left at the window

First off, a few facts most people know: that the first Nobel Prize was awarded in the Grand Hotel's Hall of Mirrors. That said hall of mirrors was inspired by the famous Galerie des Glaces in Versailles. That to this day Nobel laureates reside at the Grand Hotel and are given their own concierge. That rock stars, politicians and crowned heads bed down in incomparably luxurious suites – all this is well-known. And all this makes the Grand Hotel one of the city's icons.

The wonderful thing though is that the elegant building is open to anybody. As is the custom in an establishment of this category, every guest is treated with respect. Striding past the friendly gentlemen in grey livery, across the thick carpet and up the entrance staircase one enters into the generous hall housing the reception desk. On the way at least four employees will have been passed, all offering a friendly smile or nod. After all, anyone here might just be a VIP travelling incognito.

Turning right in the hall leads into the bar, offering guests a darker area around the counter and a lighter area with broad panorama windows looking out to the harbour. The best spot to choose is the second table to the front left at the window. Try it perhaps on a Monday afternoon or another weekday when it's pleasantly empty. Sink down into the soft cushions, order a cup of tea, listen to the muted activities in the background and watch the ships docking and undocking outside the window. The setting can't be much more sophisticated in the royal palace on the opposite side of the harbour basin. It's a little like being on a plane or on a mountain, the world below looking a bit like toytown. What goes on behind the huge panels seems strangely insignificant and far away. Stay long enough and you might just convince yourself that you are indeed a star travelling incognito.

Address Södra Blasieholmshamnen 8, 11148 Stockholm-Norrmalm | Public transport Kungsträdgården (T-bana 10, 11) | Tip In the 1963 film "The Prize", a spy thriller à la Hitchcock, Paul Newman, playing the role of Andrew Craig, winner of the Nobel Prize in Literature, spent a lot of time at the Grand Hotel's bar. His preferred tipple: dry martini.

40 _ The Haga Park Shaft
What remains of a great plan

Walking over a rocky mound right in the middle of the Haga Park forest one might suddenly stumble over a gaping deep shaft that looks like the entrance to a mine.

This is where King Gustav III once planned a large stable. The water for the horses was supposed to be pumped up from the Brunnsviken by a shaft and collected in a reservoir in the forest. While the waterworks served mainly the horses, the king had more ideas. For festive occasions in the Eko Temple down in the park the water from the reservoir was supposed to splash down the rocks, to the entertainment of the guests.

Work started in 1786. Initially the plan was to build a pump house in the style of a medieval citadel up here. The king however later dropped this idea and decided to use the windmill of Kalmar Palace as a pump.

As a consequence the mill was dismantled in 1791 and its components transported to Haga.

However, this marked the abrupt end of the ambitious undertaking. When Gustav III was assassinated in 1792 during a masquerade ball the project died with him.

The shaft is not that easy to find; but those making the effort are rewarded by phenomenal views of Brunnsviken and Haga Palace.

The best starting point is the "Stallmästaregården" hotel: head left along the water into the park. To the right lies the royal cemetery and the Eko Temple where the king liked to party. Having reached the garden café "Vasaslätten Konditori", turn left at the small green house and take a dirt track. When the track forks soon after, head into the forest. After roughly five minutes there is a clearing on the left; 20 metres before reaching it head to the right across the rocks, up to the shaft.

Address Haga Park, 11347 Stockholm-Solna | Public transport Haga Södra (bus 59) | Tip Follow up an early-morning walk in Haga Park with a right royal breakfast in fine Hotel "Stallmästaregården" (Mon–Fri 6.30–10am, Sat–Sun 7.30–10.30am). The small garden pavilion is for rent – a popular location for marriage proposals.

41 The Hammarbybacke
Take a boat to the slope

Ski aficionados might wrinkle their noses when they see this hill. In truth it isn't even a real hill. While it gets cold enough for winter sports in Stockholm, there are no high slopes, forcing people to use their imagination to come up with a solution. In reality, Hammerbybacken is a waste tip in the heart of the city, 90 metres/295 feet high. Between the 1950s and the 1980s construction waste was dumped here and in 1990 the resulting mound was simply declared a skiing area, with three easy-to-medium runs and two cable lifts transporting the winter sports enthusiasts to the "summit". There is a kind of fun treadmill for children as well as a super-easy nursery slope. And the risk-taking fraternity will enjoy the ski park with ski jumps.

Taking the lift lasts not even two minutes and a seasoned skier won't take longer than that for the downhill descent. However, on a crackling cold winter's day with bright blue skies and sunshine the views of the city and beyond from here are fabulous.

Down below is the Globen events' centre on the one side, the Hammerby Sjöstad neighbourhood – built in accordance with the latest ecological guidelines – on the other. It does seem a little absurd when double or triple the amount of water assiduously saved down there using state-of-the-art technology is spewn out again by the snow cannon up here. On the other hand, those that fancy skiing for a few hours will find an urban alpine feeling on Hammerbybacken. And whoever finds ski gymnastics in the gym too boring can practise here for the next ski holiday. There is even a ski school that offers gear for hire.

Now for the cherry on the icing: in Stockholm, there is a boat to the slopes. The Ressel shipping company takes winter sports fans on the MS Emelie from Nybroviken to Hammerby with a few stops along the way.

Address Hammarby Fabriksväg 111, 12033 Stockholm-Hammarby, www.skistar.com/sv/
hammarbybacken | Public transport Nacka Sickla station (commuter train); by boat from
Nybroplan (www.ressel.se) | Opening times Opening times vary depending on the weather;
for more information visit the homepage. | Tip In spring and summer the lift and the
mountain are open to mountainbikers, who may also rent gear here.

42 — The Häringe Slott

This palace has seen some wild times

There is not exactly a shortage of palaces in Sweden. However, "Häringe Slott" exudes its very own vibes of casual elegance, luxury and glamour. No wonder really, as the former owners of the palace enjoyed immense wealth – and hedonistic pleasures.

The first to lay claim to the peninsula was a Viking called Sote in the 11th century. Since then the terrain has seen various owners and their palaces, with today's building dating back to the 17th century. In 1929 it was purchased by newspaper mogul Torsten Kreuger, who enjoyed some wild times and implemented quite a few innovations in the palace. One of them was Sweden's first outdoor pool. This included a slide that allowed the owner to reach the pool directly from the second floor. Kreuger also constructed the first mechanical bowling alley that automatically returned the balls to the players. It is still in working order. Kreuger's evening entertainment was the stuff of legends; the dishes would be served by ladies wearing nothing but a face mask.

When Kreuger found himself in fincancial dire straits he sold the palace to Axel Wenner-Gren. The founder of the Elektrolux company, who had made a fortune selling vacuum cleaners, gave it to his wife Marguerite as a present. The Wenner-Grens formed part of the international jet set, counting Greta Garbo, Josephine Baker and even Liz Taylor amongst their guests. The couple had no children but the dazzling Marguerite owned 38 dogs over the course of her life; all are buried on Häringe. Axel Wenner-Gren and his wife also found their last resting place in front of the palace.

Today, Häringe is a hotel combining the historic with the modern in its own elegant way, serving a delicious afternoon tea for instance, with home-made cakes and sandwiches. Visitors are free to wander about the palace at their leisure. Sometimes children frolicking around on the first floor starts the chandeliers on the ground floor rattling.

Address Häringeslottsväg 13741 Västerhaninge | Public transport Häringe grindar (bus 847) | Opening times Afternoon tea: Mon–Fri 2–5pm, Sat–Sun 1–5pm | Tip It's a good idea to ring ahead to make sure there's no private party scheduled at the café (tel. +468/40052310). The Wenner-Gren Center, an international centre for visiting scientists at the northern end of downtown Sveavägen shows that the industrialist invested his money in less frivolous ventures, too.

43 Hellasgården

A dip in the ice

Hellasgården , a sports and leisure facility at the heart of a huge nature reserve, draws its eminent charm from a certain old-fashionedness. And the whole thing is only a 15-minute bus ride from Stockholm's city centre.

The best time to be here, when the place is at its most beautiful, is in winter, when the simple dark-brown wooden huts that might have been standing here already in the 1960s sport thick white caps of snow. Then it's off, either renting cross-country skis and gliding through a fairy-tale forest on illuminated tracks or ice-skating for miles across frozen Lake Källtorp. Parents with their children might want to go for a spot of sleighing. Romantic winter walks are waiting for those who like it a bit more cosy and quiet. Moreover, sports anglers can look forward to a particular pleasure: ice fishing in Lake Källtorp.

Should the activites leave one frozen to the bone a sauna is waiting. Normally men and women sweat it out separately, but there are also mixed days. One way or another, there is usually a fun atmosphere with a lot of chatting and a lot of laughing across the generational divide. Once the body is really heated up and sweat is pouring off it, then it's time to step outside for a very special experience:

Stepping out into the cold wearing only spa slippers the guests leave the sauna. If it's dark the only illumination along the path down to the lake is a Christmas tree with unusual lighting. Which is probably the reason why it generally remains standing on the pier by the water until the end of February. Carefully the visitors feel their way across the slippery soil to the tip of the boards where a large hole has been cut into the ice for sauna goers to cool their heated bodies. Now all one needs is a bit of raw courage. After drawing a deep breath and stepping onto the metal rungs, just jump into the dark waters waiting below. Letting out a big yell is part of the game!

Address Ältavägen 101, 13133 Stockholm-Nacka, www.hellasgården.se | Public transport Hellasgården (bus 401) | Opening times Visit the homepage | Tip On Saturdays and Sundays there is a barbecue between midday and 3pm in Hellasgården. Either buy a sausage from the café or pay a fee and grill your own barbecue food.

44 The Hissbana Nybohov

The mysterious Liljeholmen cable car

"Hissbana", cable car, is what the signposts in the Liljeholmen underground station state. Following the signs leads the curious through a corridor into a small waiting room. Behind glass sliding doors is a rock tunnel illuminated by neon lights and equipped with overhead wire and rails. A number of passengers have already gathered there, and soon a rubber-tyred cabin comes rolling in. When the doors slide apart it somehow reminds one of skiing or hiking holidays; in any case, this means of transport brings up images of high mountains.

The small number of passengers have hardly got off when the new ones make a beeline for the few available seats. Only 35 passengers fit into the cabin. A guard, sitting a little elevated off to the side, supervises proceedings. The doors close and off it goes. The cabin is pulled up to the Nybohovsberget at a leisurely pace. In contrast to what the name might suggest, this not a mountain at all, only a slightly higher neighbourhood in the district. The difference in altitude between the underground station of Liljeholmen and the "summit" clocks an underwhelming 37 metres or 40 yards. The trip takes one minute and 40 seconds.

The cable car has been in operation since 1964 when the underground station was finished. Initially the fee was 25 öre. Today, it is free to use and the accompanying staff only protects the installations from vandalism. No-one really knows why such an elaborate construction was chosen over a simple escalator, not the friendly guard nor the press department of Stockholm's public transport network.

And that's not the only mystery surrounding this place. During the trip various cuddly toys occupying the rock niches of the tunnel pass by. A duck over here, a tiger over there, and three animals snuggling up together behind them. Who placed them there? And why? That too will probably forever remain a secret.

Hissbana
Nybohov

Address Between T-bana Liljeholmen und Nybohovsberget, Nybohovsbacken 45, 11763 Stockholm-Liljeholmen | **Public transport** Liljeholmen (T-bana 13, 14) | **Opening times** Mon–Thu 4.45am–1.03pm, Fri 4.45am–3.48pm, Sat 5.45am–3.48pm, Sun and public holidays 5.45am–1.03pm | **Tip** Located only one underground train stop away, at Bergsundsstrand beach, the Liljeholmensbad is a pretty bath house on the waters of the Liljeholmsviken. On foot it takes about a quarter of an hour to reach.

45__ The House of God
The only project of its kind world-wide

In 2011 a little girl won a competition for the most beautiful gingerbread house with a truly original model: a combination of church and mosque. Only a child's dream or something with the potential to work as a vision for the future?

Fisksätra is the most densely populated district in Sweden, with approximately the same number of Muslims and Christians living here. Created in the 1970s, the neighbourhood consists of blocks of flats comprising four or five storeys clustered around a central square with shopping centre. Now it's at this precise spot that a project is being set up that is unique world-wide: a church for Protestants, Catholics and Muslims.

According to "Guds hus" project manager Henrik Larsson there have been cooperations between the Protestant congregation of Nacka, the Catholic St Konrad's congregation and the Muslim association for the past 50 years. The idea for a shared space for worship was born when the local schools were looking for ways to convey the idea of religious tolerance to the children. In 2007 bishop Bengt Wadensjö, a very active character, was invited to talk about religion. The bishop for his part decided to ask Imam Awad Olwan to accompany him and shifted the event to the local football pitch, marking the genesis of a unique project. People of different beliefs started talking to each other.

While the "Guds hus" might not be popular with everyone, the exchange of ideas between the neighbours is a reality now. In the House of God they find help dealing with the local authorities, language classes and legal assistance. Now the project is looking to move to a proper building to house its activities. Behind the church, which is already used by both Protestants and Catholics, a mosque is going up, connected to the original building by a glass corridor. Planning permission has been obtained, now all that's missing are the last funds to make this dream a reality.

Fisksätra kyrka

Guds hus

Address Fisksätra torg, 13341 Stockholm-Fisksätra | **Public transport** Fisksätra (Saltsjöbanan); Fisksätra station (bus 465) | **Tip** During the summer months, the "Guds hus" puts on classical concerts (Thursdays at 7.30pm, www.svenskakyrkan.se).

46 __ The House of Nobility
King for a day

Pushing against the heavy wooden door in front of the impressive portal of the "Riddarhuset" at 11.28 in the morning will not have the desired effect. It remains locked. Come 11.31 and a light pressure is sufficient to swing the heavy door inward as if by magic. Visitors stand completely alone in the impressive entrance hall of the House of Nobility. Since 1626 that has been the name and headquarters of the official organisation of Swedish and Finnish nobility.

The House of Nobility formed one of the chambers of what was then the Diet of the Estates of the Realm. From 1668 onwards, the chamber convened in the House of Nobility, which today is open for visitors. With the dissolution of the Estates in 1866, the nobility lost its privileged position and no more regular sessions took place in the House of Nobility. Today the Swedish noblesse, still comprising some 700 dynasties, convenes here every three years. The lordships decide legal questions relating to the nobility and the appropriation of their association's assets to various funds and foundations. Moreover, several academies use the room for their celebrations and there are occasional concerts, too.

From Monday to Friday at lunchtime the sacred halls open to regular folk for exactly one hour. This allows visitors to imagine what it would feel like to live here. Not a living soul, be it aristocratic or bourgeois, is to be seen, not when leaving coats in the cloakroom, nor when visiting the washrooms. It's only on the first floor that a friendly attendant takes the entrance fee and hands out an information leaflet. In the famous Knights' Hall visitors are on their own again. From top to bottom the walls are covered with the Swedish noble dynasties' coat of arms, arranged in numerical order according to the year of their introduction. So why not hold the next family council in this venerable ambience and look as if you belong here? For exactly one hour only, mind.

Address Riddarhustorget 10, 10311 Stockholm-Gamla stan, www.riddarhuset.se | Public transport Gamla stan (T-bana 13, 14, 17, 18, 19) | Opening times Mon–Fri 11.30am–12.30 pm | Tip Both at lunchtime and in the evening, concerts fitting various budgets are performed in the Riddarhuset.

47__ The Hudiksvallsgatan
Strolling through Stockholm's Chelsea

The former industrial building designed by architect Ragnar Öst-berg in Hudiksvallsgatan is an eldorado for fans of modern art. Vari-ous galleries have opened up in this red-brick ensemble dating back to the 1930s. Some have in the meantime also opened branch-es in the neighbouring streets of Gävlegatan and Hälsingegatan. Due to the many exhibitions those in the know call the Hudiksvalls-gatan – with a nod to New York's gallery district – "Stockholm's Chelsea". So between Wednesdays and Saturdays, instead of visit-ing a museum, why not enjoy a nice culture-vulture stroll through the galleries?

The walk starts at Gävlegatan 12 with the "Mia Sundberg Gallery", famous for discovering interesting new talent, some fresh from art school. Next door, number 10b houses the "Anna Thulin Gallery". Turning left behind the gallery into Hudviksvallsgatan, the first place you'll find on the left-hand side is the "Nordenhake Gallery". Going through the door marked 8 to the right of the en-trance will take the interested art goer to a set of stairs leading to the "Christian Larsen Gallery" on the first floor as well as to "Andréhn-Schiptjenko" on the second floor. These two exhibition spaces show highly unusual work by international artists.

From there just take the stairs down again and leave the building in the direction of the parking deck. On the right is "Brandstrom Stockholm", the first gallery to move to this area in 2005.

For those with enough energy left it might be worthwhile to look for the "Gallery NAU", back in Hudiksvallsgatan, next to the exit gate at 4b. The agency offers assistance to young artists taking their first steps in the art market and presents their work here in the gallery. Last but not least, following the street further to the corner with Hälsingegatan leads to the gallery "Cecilia Hillström" on the left, which shows contemporary art and photography.

Matthias van Arkel
Loop

Address Hudiksvallsgatan, 11330 Stockholm-Vasastan | Public transport Odenplan station (T-bana 17, 18, 19); Vanadisplan (bus 65, 591, 593) | Opening times Core hours Wed–Fri 12 midday–6pm, Sat 12 midday–4pm | Tip 2.5 kilometres/1.5 miles away, at John Ericssonsgatan 6, the friendly "Petite France" café serves excellent French breads and pastries as well as sandwiches.

48__ The Ivar Los Park
Playground with a view

It seems as if the tall red board fence was put there to hide a private property. But stepping through the gate you'll find yourself standing on a playground.

To the left a small boy is riding a merry-go-round, two girls are clambering around on a climbing frame and behind them children are working the swings.

The right-hand side is a play area reserved for the youngest kids. A handful of women have set up a picnic on the tables and are chatting while the little ones are happily digging away in the sand pit and having fun on the slide.

For those who have come here without children a small cobbled square behind the play area offers a few benches. They provide fabulous views across the Riddarfjärden of Kungsholmen and Gamla Stan.

The two 18th-century houses that originally stood on this plot were torn down in the 1930s. Fortunately the resulting gap was never closed with new buildings but converted into this playground with the finest view in Stockholm. And somehow the little park seems to recall times long past.

The name of this place is no less ununsual: Ivar Los Park. Ivar Lo-Johansson is considered one of the most important working-class writers of the past century. His vivid descriptions were an inspiration for quite a few fellow authors. But what links such a serious man to this playground? For 56 years, the writer lived right across from the park on the other side of the Bastugatan. When he died in 1990, it was decided to name the playground after him and to honour him with a bust.

The latter now stands on a plinth next to the sand pit, where the famous man can enjoy the children's laughter as well as the fantastic views.

Address Bastugatan 26, 11825 Stockholm-Södermalm | Public transport Mariatorget
(T-bana 13, 14; bus 43, 55, 191, 192) | Opening times Always accessible | Tip Opposite
the park, at Bastugatan 21, lies the one-bedroom flat where Ivar Lo-Johansson lived from
1934 onward; it is now a museum and open to the public.

49__ The Järva Discgolf Park
Teeing off has never been cooler

A frisbee golf course? To many that will sound like a joke, or at least like a bit of an eccentric pastime. This impression is supported by a glance at the website of the "Järva Discgolf Park". No membership nor handicap is required. The place stays open until half an hour before sunset. And if visitors want to play golf before eleven in the morning, score cards and pens are available in the white box at the car park. Payment can wait.

The gravel track running between multi-lane motorways seems to lead nowhere and does nothing to dispel apprehensions. However, after a bend to the left there is a little forest and sure enough, beyond it a rolling park landscape of well-kept cropped lawns opens up. A proper golf course.

The club house however is more reminiscent of a beach bar. The clientele fits that brief too – cool surfer types in t-shirts and shorts, all fit-looking and in good shape. The bags they carry over their shoulders containing a wide range of frisbee discs in different colours leaves no doubt: these guys mean business.

Disc golfers are friendly and happy to provide tips: beginners should under no circumstances use a cheap frisbee, but rent a professional disc. What counts they say is the flight path. A round of golf comprises 27 holes and is some four kilometres or 2.5 miles long. The starting point is the tee-off mark and the aim is to "putt" the frisbee into a basket using the least possible number of throws. Looking like a chainmail wastepaper basket, this stops the flight of the disc. Before getting there though the disc has to sail around trees and shrubs. While every disc lands in the basket at some point, with beginners this can take its time. Only constant training takes you to world-cup level. However those who find the whole thing too strenuous might prefer to enjoy a stroll across the perfectly groomed lawn.

Address Akallalänken 10, 16474 Kista, www.discgolfpark.com | **Public transport** Hjulsta (T-bana 10) | **Opening times** Mon–Fri noon–8pm, Sat–Sun 11am–6pm | **Tip** The club house hires out professional frisbees so there's no excuse not to play a round!

50___The Judarskogen

A place for geologists and mushroom hunters

Most people know the Judarskogen natural reserve for its geological formations, with traces of an Ice Age glacier that pulled back from here some 11,000 years ago.

Tensions in the ice layer and rock strata have resulted in heavy earth tremors. The deposit of Ice Age debris created a moraine six metres (nearly 20 feet) high which to this day runs through the Judarskogen over a length of several hundred yards and was named after the person who discovered it, Swedish geologist de Geer. Moreover, various sharp-edged boulders bear testimony to the tectonic shifts of the time.

There is another reason though for visiting Judarskogen: from September onwards, the trumpet chanterelle, Trattkantarell in Swedish, starts, well, mushrooming, in the moist forest around the lake. On an early autumn morning the forest is shrouded in mist, and dank cold creeps up the trousered legs. The rays of the low-hanging sun fall through the branches of trees and let the wet moss – sprinkled with spots of colour from the last blueberries and mountain cranberries – sparkle on the stones.

These are the perfect conditions for the trumpet chanterelle which loves moss, whether on tree stumps or alongside lichens on tree trunks.

To find it one needs to leave the trail and head into the forest a bit. The yellow-brownish mushroom has a distinguishing mark: the depression in its curled cap. Some grow in colonies, covering the entire forest floor. Beginners might find it hard to tell the diminutive mushroom caps from the colourful autumn leaves and might destroy an entire small colony with a single footstep. However, the hunt is well worth it. The trumpet chanterelle has a slightly peppery taste and in contrast to the real chanterelle may be easily dried and even frozen.

Address Judarskogen, 16839 Stockholm-Bromma | Public transport Ängbyplan
(T-bana 17, 18, 19) | Tip These mushrooms taste wonderful sauteed in butter with
some chopped onions, salt and pepper. Add a little crème fraîche at the end and serve
them on toasted white bread.

51__ The Konsthall C

A laundry room as art project

"Konsthall C" is the name of a non-commercial art gallery in Höka-rängen, amidst a 1940s residential neighbourhood. It's not only the location that's unusual though, but the place itself: this is the former laundry room of the neighbourhood.

A typically Swedish institution, it's a facility where residents wash their laundry in communal washing machines before drying, ironing or pressing it there. In 2004 artist Per Hasselberg, with the support of the local council, converted the laundry into a gallery – a public art project.

The Konsthall C features a permanent exhibition on the architect David Helldén, who was a major force behind the district's layout. The building also houses a district archive, and changing exhibitions are put on, some of them extremely avant-garde. Some voiced reservations at first whether a modern art gallery would be accepted in this part of town.

However, the Konsthall C was successful in gaining the support of the local residents for the project by choosing the subjects of the exhibitions wisely. Visions of the future or societal options and alternative ways of living today are subjects that interest the people here.

Hökarängen itself was once considered modern and visionary. The architecture of the buildings and the establishment of neighbourhood councils were supposed to promote communication amongst the residents.

Today, it befalls the Konsthall C and its exhibitions to stimulate the exchange of ideas. The "Centrifug" spin dryer also makes its own contribution: anyone can present their art in the small gallery within the Konsthall C. In this side room next to the laundry rather than booking washing time residents book an exhibition slot. Other parts of the building are still used as a laundry.

KONSTHALL C

Address Cigarrvägen 16, 12357 Stockholm-Farsta | Public transport Hökarängen
(T-bana 18; bus 172, 173, 182, 193) | Opening times Tue 1–8pm, Sat–Sun midday–
5pm | Tip Five minutes away, the Hökarängsplan was Sweden's first pedestrianised area,
inaugurated in 1952. The names of the shops are still designed using the curved neon
letters popular in the 1950s.

52 The Kristallvertikalaccent
No shine, no sparkle

At night, the 27m/89-feet obelisk, made up of 80,000 glass prisms, doesn't look half bad. And at Christmas time when sparkly little fir trees and deer adorn the fountain around it, it acquires a near-magical quality. In the daytime however, the problem becomes fairly obvious: this is when the glass column on Sergels torg appears simply grubby and ugly. There are those who call it a monument to failed architecture. Let's just say the original plan was very different.

When the Kristallvertikalaccent was inaugurated on Sergels torg in 1974, the idea was for the obelisk to lend some glamour to this central square. The object by glass designer Edvin Öhrström seemed to fit the superelliptical shape of the square as well as the glass facade of the Kulturhuset.

Unfortunately from day one the sculpture failed to have the impact the artist had intended for it. The original plan involved having a constant stream of water flowing down the obelisk and to provide the surrounding facades with a special light installation. Their mirror effect was supposed to make the crystal column glitter and sparkle. Yet neither the water nor the light feature were ever installed. It took until 1993 for halogen lamps to be fitted within the sculpture, lighting up the obelisk from inside. It's still not sparkling though. Rather, the effect is of a grey grubby glass pillar with a few bulbs screwed in.

It looks as if the gifted designer Edvin Öhrström had little experience dealing with projects of this size. He simply miscalculated the way the light would refract in the glass prisms. Left as it is, the column will never sparkle and shine.

However, as the city's attitude towards its buildings and monuments has radically changed since the old Klara neighbourhood was torn down, the obelisk is today considered a cultural monument and is staying as it is.

Address Sergels torg, 11157 Stockholm-Norrmalm | Public transport T-Centralen
(T-bana 10, 11, 13, 14, 17, 18, 19); Stockholm Sergels torg spårv (tram 7) | Tip Just around
the corner, at the Hötorget, is the famous concert hall where the Nobel Prizes are awarded
every year.

53__ Lånegarderoben

Borrow clothes the way you would library books

"Shareconomy" is the name of this new trend. Knowledge and music are shared online, whilst city dwellers share cars and flats. So why not clothes?, was the thinking of a few women friends from Stockholm. Do people have to actually own clothing? According to a study by Cambridge University this question makes a lot of sense. It found that women buy some 30 kilos of clothes every year, producing about the same amount of textile waste. In 2010, in an attempt to counter this trend, the young ladies founded "Lånegarderoben".

On the lower ground floor of a house in quiet picturesque Midsommarkransen, blouses, trousers, skirts and dresses from current collections hang on racks the way they would in a boutique, with a few fine vintage pieces in amongst them. Instead of price labels the clothes are marked with an inventory code. After they have paid a small contribution, members may rent up to three items of clothing per month.

The friends quickly garnered the support of textile manufacturers. Today some 20 Swedish fashion brands provide pieces from past as well as current collections in various sizes, famous brands such as Filippa K or J. Lindberg amongst them. For those who really fall in love with a piece, they can purchase it from a shop of the respective designer. Which is how they themselves benefit from this concept as well.

Lånegarderoben currently has about 350 members, 100 of whom regularly borrow clothing. Users often get chatting and tell each other how and for what occasion they wore a particular piece. In this way, the clothes acquire a history.

So far the monthly contributions cover the running costs of the shop whilst the staff are volunteers. Yet it can only be a question of time until scores of adventurous fashion fans hit Midsommarkransen.

LÅNEGARDEROBEN

Address Svandammsvägen 10, 12634 Stockholm-Midsommarkransen | **Public transport** Midsommarkranksen (T-bana 14) | **Opening times** Thu 5–8pm, last Sat of the month midday–4pm | **Tip** Right next door, in house number 8, "Lyckliga Gatan-Vintage Kuriosa Design" sells vintage and branded clothing, furniture, lamps and curiosities.

54__ The Laundry Museum
Washing like great-grandma

In the early 20th century there were hundreds of laundries in the Huddinge area south of Stockholm. The numerous lakes and brooks in the surroundings attracted the small businesses. The whole family would scrub and help out. Once a week the freshly washed and ironed washing was returned to the clients in Stockholm by horse-drawn cart and dirty washing taken on board.

One of the first laundries belonged to the Johansson family and was located in Masmovägen on the Albysjön. This is where artist Olle Magnusson opened Sweden's first and so-far only laundry museum in 1994.

With a lot of sense for detail he made the arduous day-to-day life of the washer families come to life again. On a little jetty on the water stands a tin vat with laundry bats and brush alongside. A fire emitting copious quantities of smoke burns underneath a huge boiler.

On a guided tour the museum's director demonstrates how the old equipment was used. Forcefully he stirs the contents of the vat with a dolly. Then he fishes out a dripping wet pair of long johns, throws them onto a washboard, adds liquid soap, scrubs the fabric energetically with a brush and pulls the underpants through the water once more. Eventually he feeds them through a small wooden mangle that was supposed to facilitate the wringing-out of the washing. As he goes along Magnusson reveals how farms were worked at the time.

On the washing lines behind the house old-fashioned white bodices and bedlinen are drying in the sun. Washing machines from various decades are exhibited inside the house, dating from the mid-19th century. One room shows only antique irons which did actually consist of iron and had to be heated above a fire. All of this makes our own household work appear child's play by comparison.

Address Masmovägen 20–22, 14332 Vårby, www.ollemagnusson.se | Public transport Masmo (T-bana 13; bus 172, 740, 865) | Opening times One Sun in the month in spring and autumn, for groups by appointment, Olle Magnusson, tel. 08/7742227 or 070/3206892, olle@ollemagnusson.se | Tip The bright main building houses the "Vårby-Fittja Fittja" local association. When the museum is open, there is coffee and cake for sale.

55 __ The Lunch Beat

A lunch break with a difference at Kulturhuset

It all started in a car park below Stockholm's Hötorget. In summer 2010, 14 people who fancied doing something different to relax from work during their lunch break got together there. They set up a ghetto blaster, dancing exuberantly for one hour to loud music.

This marked the birth of the Lunch Beat. The idea of Stockholm-based Molly Ränge spread like wildfire. These days, once a month some 1000 people groove to the beat in Stockholm's Kulturhuset.

The crowd is quite diverse: young gentlemen in well-fitting suits alongside older ladies in a two-piece and casually dressed 20-year olds stream into the hall that is illuminated by colourful lights. The ghetto blaster has now been replaced by DJs who fire up the dancers to their best ability. Whereas it can take a while for things to get going in nightclubs, at the Lunch Beat revellers hit the floor immediately. People come here for one thing only: to dance. Everybody can wriggle off their worries, let their souls recover and refuel on new energy.

Apparently the effects are so positive that some superiors make a point of sending their staff to the Lunch Beat. To spare the dance aficionados hunger pangs at work later on, sandwiches are provided. Alcohol is taboo.

The idea has now spread across the whole world. In 2013, the first Lunch Beats took place in New York and Montreal. Which is why Molly Ränge and her friends have now drawn up a few Lunch Beat rules. Profiting from the events is frowned upon; commercial event organisers or firms are subject to strict rules.

The Lunch Beat always has to be announced publicly and be accessible to everyone. Sponsors are allowed to support the meetings discreetly by supplying a sound system or providing organic snacks. Enjoy!

Address Sergels torg, 11157 Stockholm-Norrmalm, www.Lunchbeat.org | Public transport T-Centralen (T-bana 10, 11, 13, 14, 17, 18, 19); Stockholm Sergels torg (tram 7) | Tip The first Lunch Beat in the car park "Lunch Beat Stockholm #1" is on You Tube.

56_ The Mangling room
Let the fabrics shine

This small mangling operation occupies the unobtrusive basement of a block of flats on Östermalm. From the outside it's difficult to guess at the cultural treasure hiding inside. Here the laundry is still pressed the way it used to be over a century ago. Two huge box mangles dating back to 1886 fill nearly the entire room.

A box or stone mangle works without heat, smoothing the washing by sheer force. For this, the pieces of washing, dry or a little moist, are wrapped across a cylindrical wooden roller, with the help of a special linen mangle cloth, which requires a certain dexterity. Afterwards the roller is placed inside the mangle, where it is moved backward and forwards between a stone plate and a box filled with stones and pieces of iron. Faced with this kind of weight creases do not stand a chance. In the past the rollers were moved by hand; today the whole operation is run electronically.

The last owner was mangling laundry for the people of Östermalm over a period of 50 years. When she retired in 2001 at over 80 years of age the place was supposed to be shut down and replaced by a bike shop.

But Britt Marie Soler didn't want that to happen. The petite elderly lady lives in the neighbourhood, working as a secretary in a law firm. When she heard about the impending closure she resolved on the spur of the moment to take over the business. Britt Marie reduced her working hours in the office and started mangling for two half days a week.

The stone mangle treats fine fabrics gently, lending them an incomparable shine, the owner reveals, proudly presenting a freshly mangled piece of silk. There are plenty of pretty fabrics in the wealthy Östermalm households. Britt Marie's services are sought after to the point that she now has to set the antique machines to work for an additional day.

Address Banérgatan 33, 11522 Stockholm-Östermalm | Public transport Karlaplan
(T-bana 13; bus 42, 44) | Opening times Mon–Tue 10am–2pm, Thu 1–6pm | Tip
The Japanese restaurant "EDO" around the corner, at Linnégatan 38, serves excellent
food at fair prices. The welcoming owner Li Hua Zhou is more than happy to fulfil special
requests.

57 — The Mosque
Just relax for a moment

Right across the entrance is a "reception", where a friendly gentleman helps visitors overcome any initial reservations. The warm welcome is surprising; in the past the mosque had some bad press for its alleged support for suicide attacks and anti-American agitation. Yet there is certainly no prejudice against western visitors.

Everybody is welcome, no part is off limits. All women have to do is put on a long thin hooded cloak. But not to worry, these are available on site.

In the prayer room the iron girders under the high ceiling serve as a reminder of the industrial past of this listed building. The structure used to house a power plant that provided electricity for the Stockholmers. Around the turn of the century architect Ferdinand Boberg was one of the stars of his trade. As was the fashion at the time, he added Oriental elements to the building, even orienting it towards Mecca. When in the late 1990s the need arose to find a place for a new mosque, Katarinenstationen was the perfect fit.

Today, the former factory building is carpeted. A handful of men are napping in one corner, others sit next to them, legs crossed, chatting. Scattered over the rest of the room some faithful are praying. A shopping bag next to them, their smartphone in front, they have stopped here for a quick break. This brings the ambience fairly close to the character of the initial prayer space created by Muhammad. The Prophet intended the mosque to be a space not only for prayer, but also to promote social contacts and further education. Viewed from this perspective a mosque is a political and social hub too.

The women's prayer room is located on the first-floor gallery. Here again the welcome is warm and visiting women can discover completely new opportunities to escape the shopping rage for a while.

Address Kapellgränd 10, 11625 Stockholm-Södermalm | Public transport Medborgarplatsen (T-bana 17, 18, 19; buses 59, 66, 193, 194, 195, 791, 794) | Tip Legendary football player Lennart Skoglund used to live on Katarina bangata 42. A monument standing across the street was set up in his honour.

58 The Museum Flat
Back to the 1960s

A grey rotary dial telephone stands on a small table in the hallway. Flower-printed curtains hang outside the windows, and a green-patterned wax tablecloth covers the kitchen table. The cupboards are full of original packaging from the 1960s. An old index-card box holds recipes, amongst them tips for treats like a "Coffee-table Spread With a Difference". In the living room visitors can spot the record "The Best of Tom Jones", and a wildly patterned towelling robe in pink and orange hangs in the guest WC.

We are in the flat of the Artursson family. The year is 1969, when the first manned mission to the moon took place, Olof Palme became prime minister, Swedish television had all of two channels and the Stockholm government made the ambitious plan to build a million flats within ten years. Every citizen of Stockholm was supposed to be provided with an affordable and comfortable home. It was as part of this drive that the suburb of Tensta (see page 208) was realised in the northwest part of Stockholm. At the time Irene and Sven Artursson were one of the first families to move into the 85-square-metre three-room flat with their three children. In Småland they had paid more for less space. Tensta promised modern life with all comforts and an underground link to Stockholm's city centre.

Some 45 years later Tensta is considered a "problematic neighbourhood" with a soaring unemployment rate and a high proportion of ethnic minorities. Not much has remained of the optimism of the early years. In order to allow visitors to experience the ambience of the time when the future was looking bright, as well as the way things have changed since then, Stockholm's Stadsmuseum carried out an unusual project in 2006. With the help of Irene Artursson her flat was reverted to its original state, offering an interesting time-travel experience. To make the whole thing more authentic there are plans to offer evening cookery courses with typical dishes of that era.

Address Kämpingebacken 13, 16368 Stockholm-Spånga | Public transport Tensta (T-bana 10) | Opening times Visits can only be arranged for groups; for bookings ring tel. +468/50831620 | Tip Stockholm's Stadsmuseum has set up a total of four flats from various eras for the general public (for information on guided tours visit www.stadsmuseum.stockholm.se).

59 — The National City Park

A national park with factories and an urban motorway

Covering an area of 27 square kilometres/ten square miles, it forms a green ribbon snaking its way right through the city. Yet some 30 per cent of the Stockholmers aren't aware of it. This seems strange, as the Kungliga Nationalstadsparken or Ekoparken was the first of its kind in the world. The principles of the national city park are inscribed on a massive granite block standing like a monument at the entrance to the Hagaparken. Moreover, the stone also shows visitors the region comprised by this urban national park, stretching from Skeppsholmen and Fjäderholmen all the way to Sörentorp. The Djurgården, Haga and Ulriksdal parks form part of it, the latter including Lake Brunnsviken as well as the swamp tract of Uggleviken, an area of great ecological interest.

Foxes, badgers, martens, minks, deer and elk, as well as hundreds of types of birds, unusual insects and plants are found in the Ekoparken. Yet the area not only includes natural landscapes but also industrial facilities, modern housing developments, the university and even an inter-urban motorway. Castles and museums complement the picture.

But what does national city park actually stand for? Going back to an initiative by the Swedish king Carl XVI Gustaf, the project was realised in December 1994 by a Reichstag resolution. The law demands that the terrain of the national city park must remain unaltered just as it was originally in 1994. Within its boundaries, new buildings or other drastic changes are only permitted in exceptional cases and any change must not have an adverse affect the historic landscape, its natural or cultural values.

However, the project does not only have supporters. Critics claim the Ekoparken has impeded the city's development and growth. What is certain is that the area offers visitors a unique blend of natural and cultural experiences, among them the fine Ulrikdal Palace, botanical gardens and the Butterfly House.

NATIONALSTADSPARKEN ULRIKSDAL – HAGA –

Address Between Annerovägen and Brunnsviksvägen next to Stallmästaregården, 11347 Stockholm-Solna | Public transport Haga Södra (bus 59, 73) | Tip 2010 saw the inauguration of a 36-kilometre bike trail, leading through the Ekoparken from Ulriksdal in the north to Blocksudden in the south. Small grey signs featuring a white bike point the way.

60_Nelly Sachs' Flat

A very special literary monument

The Royal Library collects everything that has been printed in Sweden since 1661 – from the telephone directory to hand-written documents and decrees issued by the royal family. It also collects posters and paintings and boasts an extensive audiovisual collection. Lying hidden 30 metres below the surface is a very special treasure: the flat of poet Nelly Sachs. Born 1891 in Berlin, the German-Jewish writer first made a name for herself in Germany during the 1920s. In 1940 Swedish author Selma Lagerlöf helped Nelly Sachs to flee from the Nazis to Stockholm, where she would live up to her death in 1970.

Visiting the flat that occupies some 40 square metres/430 square feet it becomes clear that the great poet lived modestly: a blue sofa with matching armchair in the style popular during the 1940s; an overflowing bookshelf with works by authors ranging from Kafka to Wittgenstein; in front of it a pink-coloured tray full of stones and shells; around the corner, the bedroom that once included a kitchenette.

Visitors can leaf through the author's poetry albums and picture cards collection and look into her sowing kit. In the bedroom is the typewriter used by the poet to translate Swedish poetry into German, in order to earn a livelihood for herself and her sick mother.

With her own work, Nelly Sachs highlighted the suffering caused by the Holocaust and the survivors' feeling of guilt. In 1966, Sachs shared the Nobel Prize for Literature with Shmuel Yosef Agnon, donating the prize money to the disadvantaged. Following her death the heirs left her flat to the Royal Library, which used both the furniture and her works to create this unique monument to the poet.

Address Humlegården, 10241 Stockholm-Östermalm | Public transport Östermalmstorg
(T-bana 13, 14) | Opening times Every first Wed in the month at 2pm or by appointment,
email info@kb.se | Tip Take the opportunity to stroll through the Humlegården and study
sculptures of famous Swedish scientists and writers.

61_ The Norrskär

The elegant way of travelling to the Schärgarten

The majestic old steamer lies at anchor at the Strömkajen pier; hull and railing shine in flawless white, the wheelhouse on the bridge deck gleams in exotic wood. Instead of modern PVC fenders, halved tree trunks prevent the boat's hull from damage during docking manoeuvres. Built in 1910 in Göteborg as a passenger boat for the Seippelt shipping company, the steamer initially transported the first Stockholmers into the Schärengarten under the name of "Sandhamns Express". Both artists and industrialists felt the pull of the sea and nature's charms, without wanting to forego luxury however on their way. Time was passed in style in the drawing room and with fine dining in the restaurant. The Norrskär was regarded as the most beautiful and elegant steam-ship of its time. In 1947 the municipal shipping company Waxholmsbolage became the new owner and gave it the name it carries today.

At weekends, the steamer still covers the route to Sandhamn in 3.5 hours at an unhurried pace, on weekdays it continues all the way to Vaxholm. The original steam engine continues to pound away in the ship's belly after more than 100 years. Guests with an interest in technology have the opportunity of visiting the engine room free of charge. Sitting on the red plush benches in the drawing room immediately takes passengers back to times long gone by. Here too the wooden panelling is polished till it shines and the staff wear fancy uniforms.

The restaurant bar though is a recent invention, as alcohol was originally banned during the cruise. Otherwise everything is as it used to be in the olden days: plenty of wood and brass, white tablecloths, small vases with lovingly arranged little flowers in between. Only the slightly askew lampshades appear a little wobbly, which only serves to enhance the overall charm. Reserving a table is advisable. One speciality is the famous Ångbåtsbiff, the steamer steak, which was in former times actually fried on top of the red-hot ship boiler.

Address Strandvägen, 11487 Stockholm-Östermalm | Public transport Kungsträdgården
(T-bana 10, 11; for information on "steamboat-tours" see www.waxholmsbolaget.se) | Tip
At Strandvägen 29–33, the Bünsowska Hus was built between 1886 and 1888 for millionaire
Friedrich Bünsow. Behind the facade, reminiscent of a French Loire castle, there are three
large houses comprising a number of upmarket flats.

62__Nystekt Strömming
So simple yet so good

The little snack van looks a little lost on the large square in front of the exit of Slussen underground station. Snow, rain or sunshine, "Nystekt Strömming" is always open. The place only closes once a year, on 1 January.

The yellow sign in the shape of a fish reveals what the visitor can expect: freshly fried strömming. This is a herring species only found in the Baltic Sea with sizes reaching from 15 to 24 centimetres; its Atlantic cousins measures some 30 centimetres.

The van serves Strömming with crispbread (aka knäckebröd) or rye bread, with mashed potatoes, onions, beetroot, carrots, garlic or mustard sauce. And this herring tastes just superb in any variation, a fact appreciated by business people from the surrounding offices as much as the passers-by suffering sudden hunger pangs during a shopping spree or travellers changing at the Slussen transport hub.

At lunchtime a longish queue forms around the small van. But any other time too a handful of customers line up along the narrow counter. The whole thing is all the more surprising as one eats standing up in any weather with only a very basic shelter.

Up until six years ago the snack bar belonged to a Swede. When he retired, the Egyptian Mohammed Karam took over the business, paying for his predecessor's recipes and a period of training on the job. Which is why the mashed potato still has this incomparably creamy consistency which results from a dab of butter. The skin of the Strömming is fried to a crisp finish and the salads are fresh and crunchy.

For 23 long years the small van was the only place in Stockholm offering fried strömming. Now a cousin of the current owner opened a branch in Kista, making the locals there well happy with anticipation.

Address Södermalmstorg 1, 11645 Stockholm-Södermalm | Public transport Slussen
(T-bana 13, 14, 17, 18, 19; tram 25, 26) | Opening times daily 10am – 10pm | Tip The
neighbouring Stadsmuseum has a playroom for children which looks like Old Stockholm,
complete with an olde-worlde shop, harbour and market.

63__ Och Himlen därtill
The sky comes for free …

"Skrapan" it says in orange and yellow neon lighting above the entrance. Inside, the first impression is that of a fairly unspectacular shopping mall with neon lighting and various boutiques. Then, an elevator tucked away in the back corner whisks visitors up to one of the coolest places in Stockholm, with breathtaking views.

When the building – designed by architect Paul Hedqvist – was completed in 1959, its 81 metres/266 feet made it the tallest building in Sweden. In 1964 the Dagens Nyheter Tower eclipsed it by three metres.

The uninviting area in front of the elevator as well as the sober car itself serve as a reminder that the Stockholm Inland Revenue Office was housed here until 2003.

When the tax people moved out, a large part of the building was converted into a student hall of residence, adding two storeys in the process. This is why the original elevator only goes up to the 25th instead of the 27th floor. A flight of stairs brings visitors up to the top.

This part of the house has a glass facade, so fantastic views open up on the last flight of stairs already – which might make it a bit of a challenge for people suffering from vertigo. The staircase ends in an elegant bar that offers a sensational panorama in all directions. From here it's possible to look across the complete city with its old, new, beautiful and sometimes ugly houses, its endless expanses of water, countless parks and widespread transport network; and further even beyond the city limits.

The clientele here is mixed: young women taking a drink after work, young men casually dressed in jeans and t-shirt drinking beer, and men in suits plying their business partners with the view. Drinks and snacks aren't exactly cheap, but the views are worth it. And the sky comes for free.

Address Götgatan 78, 11830 Stockholm-Södermalm | **Public transport** Medborgarplatsen (T-bana 17, 18, 19) | **Opening times** Mon–Thu 5pm–1am, Fri–Sat 4pm–3am, entrance reserved to the over-25s | **Tip** On Saturdays from 10am to 3pm there is a farmer's market along Katarina bangata, selling organic produce.

64_ Öja
The most hospitable island in the Skärgården

A first glance leaves little doubt: this is a place where the world is still intact. A handful of colourful wooden houses cluster around the harbour basin of Öja, and the island dwellers offer guests a friendly welcome on arrival.

But walking towards the oldest lighthouse in Sweden might leave visitors feeling a little confused: on the rocks, fat old cannons shine in the sun. A panel explains that an important World War II military post was located here. However, fortunately nothing serious happened during the war: Once, warning shots were fired at a supposedly German plane, which turned out to be a Swedish one. A Stockholm superintendent suspecting an illegal distillery on the island found nothing. And eventually a ship ran aground here and sank. Not through enemy fire, but because the captain was temporarily blinded. No one was harmed.

A four kilometre/2.5-mile gravel road connects the south of the narrow island with the north. This is where visitors can find untouched, unspoilt nature. Sculptures and information panels provide a little diversion and ensure that things do not get too monotonous. Any attraction, small as it may be, is proudly presented. And the ubiquitous rocks invite visitors to take some time for a spot of undisturbed sunbathing and a dip in the sea.

This idyll is slightly disturbed though by the somewhat surreal sign pointing to a military museum. The museum houses a dinosaur-like object – an anti-aircraft rocket weighing twelve tons. Visitors may also visit a four-storey underground defensive facility. During the Cold War, Öja was one of the six major military bases supposed to protect Sweden in the event of a Soviet attack. The whole thing was so secret that foreigners have only been allowed onto the island since 2000. Maybe this explains this feeling that the island dwellers are truly pleased about every visitor.

Address Öja, 14995 Nynäshamn | Public transport Commuter train 35 to Nynäshamn, then bus 852 to Torö, getting off at Ankarudde | Tip The small supermarket at Skravleviken marina rents out accommodation and serves food. Lucky ones will have the seats between the rocks all to themselves, to enjoy a delicious fish soup maybe?

65 __ The Östermalms IP
Lunch-break skating

Located next to the impressive Olympic stadium by architect Torben Grut, constructed with 400,000 hand-made bricks and still boasting the original royal box with its pretty wooden canopy, Östermalms IP looks modest at first glance. However, when the sports grounds were personally inaugurated by none other than Oscar II in 1906, the facility was considered very modern for its time, even serving as a venue for the 1912 Olympic Games. The winners in the disciplines riding, fencing and tennis were victorious here, with baseball games taking place, too.

Today, mainly football is played on Östermalms IP. In the summers between 2005 and 2007 the gravel-covered grounds also served as a temporary campsite. The best thing about this place however is that since 1970 the 400-metre running track has been turned into a fantastic ice rink every winter. As the ice is made and maintained by underground cooling coils, skaters can reliably come here for their rounds even in milder winters and up until eleven o'clock at night. This is the only circular ice rink in town, perfectly suited to proper skating. The central location also allows employees from the surrounding area to swap their business dress for sports gear and fine leather shoes for some blades during lunch break.

On the occasion of the rink's 40th anniversary a special event took place. Ice hockey matches had been held here as early as the 1920s, and ice-hockey clubs had already been pushing for a repeat of such a tournament. In the particularly cold winter of 2010/2011 their moment had come. The oval was flooded with water and the two big clubs, Djurgården IF Bandy and AIK stepped up to a legendary match. The snow flurry was so intense that the game had to be interrupted several times, eventually taking three hours instead of one. Still, many are rooting for a repeat performance.

Address Fiskartorpsvägen 2, 11433 Stockholm-Östermalm | **Public transport** Stadion
(T-bana 14); Östermalms Idrottsplats (bus 55) | **Opening times** Mon–Fri 9am–4pm and
5pm–11pm, Sat and Sun to 9pm; for enquiries about skates rental: tel. +468/50828354 |
Tip At weekends barbecues are set up along the rink. From midday onwards ice skaters
can fortify themselves with hot dogs and the like.

66_ The Park Theatre
Old-fashioned thespian art

Strolling along on a summer's evening from the T-bana station Skanstull via Ringvägen or from Ljusterögatan in the direction of Vitabergsparken, you're likely to meet a lot of people carrying picnic hampers. The more elegant ones might feature a bottle of wine peaking out from under the clean dish cloth. In the more down-to-earth ones plastic cutlery joins bottled beer, large chunks of cheese and bread. And those who didn't have time to organise any food might be seen carrying a plastic bag with sushi from the Asia snack bar around the corner. Their destination is the open-air stage in Vitabergsparken.

The Parkteatern as it's called here can look back on a long tradition. Every summer since 1942 Stockholm's Stadsteater has been putting on free open-air performances; the open-air stage in Vitabergsparken has been around since 1954. Sitting on stepped wooden benches the audience surrounds the stage. An hour before the performance begins the rows are already well filled, with people eating, drinking, chatting and laughing everywhere.

The programme is varied, from acrobatic and circus performances, concerts and opera to drama. A special children's programme is on offer too. Much of it can be enjoyed by a non-Swedish-speaking audience. And there is usually a cheerful atmosphere. This is probably how theatre would have been in the olden days, when travelling jesters entertained the people with their show.

When the performance begins, things quieten down. Everybody is watching the stage, spellbound. Behind the spotlights dusk is slowly descending on the park. A young couple starts snuggling up to each other. Children look on amazed and open-mouthed as an acrobat spins through the air. The only creature not very interested in the action is a large hunting dog sleeping next to the bench. At the end of the performance, the audience rewards the actors with calls of "bravo", the moon shining in the sky above.

Address Vitabergsparken, 11635 Stockholm-Södermalm, www.stadsteatern.stockholm.se | Public transport Skanstull (T-bana 17, 18, 19) | Tip The "Nytorget Urban Deli" at Nytorget 4 sells unusual groceries from bread and vegetables to fish and shellfish, as well as lemonades and fresh pressed juices. The associated restaurant comes recommended.

67 — The Pionen Data Centre

A place right out of a science fiction movie

In winter, white steam billows from a rock wall in Renstierna Gata below Vitaberg Park. It originates from a gigantic cooling system running behind the 40-centimetre strong glass entrance door in the rock. The word "Pionen" is affixed in blue neon writing above the entrance.

In the 1970s this was the cover name of a nuclear shelter, which the Swedish government had dynamited 30 metres deep into the stone wall. In 2006 the Swedish internet provider "Bahnhof AB" took over the military facility, setting up its largest data centre here. The result is a high-tech backdrop worthy of a film set.

Ensuring that the hundreds of servers don't overheat, the impressive cooling system is located right beyond the entrance inside a rock grotto. Next to it two diesel motors, originally developed for German U-boats, serve as emergency back-up generators. Only then does one reach the reception proper. The walls are bare rock over which lush green plants are climbing. Waterfalls splash down in between the stones. Plants also completely cover the walls in the adjacent office where 15 staff sit in front of their screens in simulated daylight.

At the heart of the facility is the server room where the data of Bahnhof AB is processed. But external companies can park their servers in the "Pionen" data centre too. Thus, the internet platform "Wikileaks" keeps its data safely stored here. A glass conference room hovers above the servers, connected to the entrance area by a glass bridge.

This would make an ideal location for a "James Bond" film, where a baddie plans to annihilate the world by cyber attack. "Pionen" would resist even an assault by a hydrogen bomb and in the case of a terror attack plans exist to have it serve as a national communications hub.

Address Renstierna Gata 37, 11631 Stockholm-Södermalm | Public transport
Medborgarplatsen (T-bana 17, 18, 19); Renstiernas gata (bus 66, 96) | Opening
times Check www.bahnhof.net for information on how to visit the data centre. |
Tip "Mormor Dumplings" at Bondegatan 58 serves dim sums on comfy wooden
tables amongst typically Asian decoration.

68 The Poetry and Relaxation Armchair

Resting in the bosom of Abraham

Built by Swedish star architect Gunnar Asplund, the city library is always worth a visit. The central section of this beautiful 1920s functionalist building is a three-storey rotunda surrounded by tall bookshelves made from noble wood. The bright ceiling lends the space an atmosphere of light and aspiration. In the centre, visitors can relax on elegant leather benches, and occasionally readings are held here.

At several points corridors lead from the rotunda into the surrounding reading rooms and specialised libraries. Everywhere you look, studious visitors are sweating over learned volumes. Surprisingly, there is a spot in this venerable place of knowledge where visitors have the opportunity and are encouraged even to indulge in wonderful relaxation: a bright red armchair, the cushions of which completely envelop the seated person. A sign encourages visitors to take a break in what is called the "Poetry and Relaxation Armchair" and to contact library staff to try it out. The charming librarians will give the relaxation seeker a small album with CDs containing Swedish poetry or meditation music. A lead connects the armchair to a – slightly old-fashioned looking – CD player.

Now all that's left to do is place the CD into the player and allow yourself to sink back into the cushions. Everything around is quickly forgotten. No earphones to press down on the ears, no bothersome lead to detract from enjoying the recording. Ever so softly, the music or poems surge out of the thick padding. The armchair usually stands at a window so one can watch the world go by in the park or on the street. Or else just close your eyes and float away into another world. Visitors are also most welcome to bring in their own favourite CD.

Address Stadsbibliotek, Sveavägen 73, 11350 Stockholm-Vasastan | **Public transport** Oden-plan (T-bana 17, 18, 19) | Opening times Mon–Fri 9am–7pm, Sat–Sun 12 midday–4pm | Tip The beautiful water fountains with small bronze sculptures visible outside the windows of the reading rooms are originals, dating back to the 1920s and definitely worth a closer look.

69 The Preem Petrol Station

Secret hipster spot on Kungsholmen

The northern banks of the Riddarfjärden in the Kungsholmen neighbourhood is a well-to-do area. Stately residences from the 1920s and 1930s occupy this location not far from the Stadshus with its famous tower.

On the Norr Mälarstrand promenade a few chic restaurants and trendy bars offer waterside food and drink. One of them is the "Orangerie", cocktail bar and café. Just as in a proper orangery lemon, orange and olive trees fill the spaces between aviaries and velvet-covered sofas and armchairs. The restaurant next door rests on pontoons that allow one to eat not only alongside but actually on the water.

A little further on however is a place that some insiders now consider to be the by far cooler location: the Preem Petrol Station. The modern facility, whose pumps and roof are painted a bright orange, also offers beautiful views. Here too diners occupy a pole position alongside the water, only the furnishings are a little more basic.

Next to the sales pavilion a large poster features bright green apples, and a few simple wooden tables with chairs and benches stand out front. The shop serves coffee in all variations, as well as muffins, filled rolls snd sandwiches. Naturally there is the complete range of products one would expect to find on the shelves of a petrol station, too.

In "Preems Café" a man in workwear sits next to an elderly lady reading the papers and enjoying a kanelbulle (cinnamon roll). At the table next door a group of young people are having a good time. None of them came here to buy petrol but for the extremely relaxed, easy-going and somehow cool ambience.

Come evening there is ample opportunity to study the current fashion trends, when the diners headed for the surrounding restaurants stroll by.

Address Norr Mälarstrand 31, 11220 Stockholm-Kungsholmen | **Public transport** Rädhuset (T-bana 10, 11); Kungsholms kyrka (bus 3, 62) | **Opening times** Mon–Sun 6am–midnight | **Tip** Walking towards the Stadshus leads to very comfortable wooden benches shaped like deckchairs with ample room to stretch out on them. They are also broad enough to support more than one person. A pretty spot for a little break with a view of the water.

70_ The Rain Shelter
Feeling like ABBA for once

Leave the Jewish Theatre on your left and cross the bridge in the direction of Djurgården, taking the first path to your right beyond the bridge. After some 200 metres you'll spot it to your left, in a meadow – the rain shelter. No wonder walkers and joggers pass by without taking further notice of it. The small, Chinese-looking shelter doesn't seem very spectacular. The fact that a photograph of this place reached great fame is due to the people who once had their picture taken here.

Björn Ulvaeus, Benny Andersson, Agnetha Fältskog and Anni-Frid Lyngstad, better known as ABBA, took some photographs here in 1970 to promote some of their planned concerts. At that point the two women were only background singers for their husbands. In June 1972 they launched their first single, called "People need Love". At the time the four had not yet formed a band and were busy with their own projects so not a lot of effort was put into releasing the single. For the cover they used the picture they had taken here two years previously for that concert under said rain shelter. The name of the band at the time was simply Björn & Benny, Agnetha & Anni-Frid.

Even if the title doesn't exactly sound like an instant number one hit it didn't harm the success of the song, which entered the Swedish charts straight after its release. And it was this hit single that prompted the two couples eventually to record an album together.

In 1974 ABBA had their international breakthrough with the song "Waterloo", which won the Eurovision Song Contest. And with the band's success, the first single with that picture of the rain shelter acquired its own share of fame.

All it takes to feel like ABBA for once is the following: take two men and two women in bell-bottoms and have them sit in each of the four corners below the rain shelter. And then just smile like a star.

Address At the start of Maniliavägen turn into the nameless path, even before you hit Rosendalsvägen, 11525 Stockholm-Djurgården | Public transport Djurgårdsbrunn (bus 69) | Tip In summer, the "Djurgårdsbrunn" bar-cum-restaurant at Djurgårdsbrunnsvägen 69 is a nice place to sit on the terrace.

71__ The Rainforest Path
A sensual experience

When hearing "rainforest" some people might think of tropical rainforests and Tarzan dangling off a liana. It's not quite like that in the rainforest at Tyresta National Park.

Still, here too after only a few minutes visitors feel completely alone, far from civilisation. Some parts of he 2.5km/1.5-mile rainforest walk, or Urskogsstigen, even lead over comfortable wooden planks. The immediate surroundings however are wild and primordial.

Everywhere you look, conifers that are hundreds of years old send their branches far up into the sky. Slim spruces grow next to gnarly old pines. Some trees lean against each other for support, bent by the wind, others line the forest floor, criss-crossed. Occasional roots peak out of the undergrowth as so many monsters.

Here no tree is felled or cleared. Dead plants offer a home to insects and birds, eventually turning into fertile forest soil. In between the trunks one can spot shiny green pillows of moss, then again rocks reminiscent of the backs of bathing hippos. There are crackling sounds everywhere; the forest is alive. All of this lends this virgin forest its incomparable beauty. Here visitors can enjoy remoteness and silence or listen to the melody of the wind in the treetops. With a little luck they might spot capercaillie cocks in the early hours, or, at dusk, admire an elk.

The landscape consists of the remains of a mountain range nearly two billion years old, converted by the forces of nature and the last Ice Age into a mainly flat plain.

In 1929 newspaper magnate Torsten Kreuger purchased the area, intending to clear it. A forest warden noticed the priceless value of the forest and informed the city of Stockholm, which saved the 2000 hectares at the last minute. The area was only declared a nature reserve in 1986.

Address Tyresta by, 13659 Vendelsö | Public transport Tyresta (bus 834) | Tip In 1999 an enormous fire destroyed a large part of the area west of Stensjön Lake. Still, many plants and animals ended up benefiting from the fire. Life again emerged between the charred tree trunks, creating a new landscape.

72__ The Raoul Wallenberg Square

Two monuments for a courageous man

In 1944 the Swedish government sent 31-year old diplomat Raoul Wallenberg to Budapest, where he dedicated himself to saving some 100,000 Jewish citizens from deportation to Auschwitz, using false Swedish passports. In 1945 the Soviet secret service kidnapped Wallenberg, suspecting him of espionage. He was to spend two years in various Soviet prisons; after 1947 the trail runs cold. The role of the Swedish government in this affair is not a particularly glorious one. Wallenberg's disappearance was ignored, as were offers on the part of the Soviet government for an exchange of prisoners. For ten years, a Soviet-Swedish research team tried to resolve Wallenberg's whereabouts, yet to this day the fate of this courageous man is unknown. So in a way it's quite fitting that Raoul Wallenberg torg on Nybroplan is not marked on many maps. On the other hand, there are actually two monuments here to this quiet hero. The twelve reclining bronze sculptures created by Danish artist Kirsten Ortwed in 2001 met with little enthusiasm. Despite the fact that Wallenberg's family was given a say in the design, on completion his sister remarked that the sculptures looked like twelve ugly stones. At least the artist cast Wallenberg's signature in bronze, as a reminder of the thousands of passports he signed that would save Hungarian Jews from the extermination camps.

This message, however, was apparently not deemed to be clear enough by the Jewish community, whose synagogue is around the corner and who therefore erected a second monument in 2006. A stone sphere bears Wallenberg's name and the phrase: "The road was straight when Jews were deported to death. The road was winding, dangerous and full of obstacles when Jews were trying to escape their murderers." A symbolic path with cobblestones from the Budapest ghetto leads from here in the direction of the synagogue.

OUL WALLENBE

Address Nybroplan, 11147 Stockholm-Östermalm | Public transport Nybroplan (tram 7, bus 52, 62, 69, 76, 91) | Tip At Gustav-Adolfs torg, right in front of the Ministry of Foreign Affairs, another monument to Raoul Wallenberg was inaugurated in 2012: a bronze diplomat's briefcase bearing the initials R. W. on a bench of black granite. A matching monument entitled "Hope" by the artist couple Kratz can be found in front of the UN Headquarters in New York.

73__Rosenhill

Emilia and Lars create their very own world

Some places are intrinsically linked to the people who conceived them. One such place is "Rosenhill". When Emilia and her husband Lars took over the century-old garden shop and nursery in the late 1990s from Emilia's parents, they converted it to organic agriculture. Since then the couple has been transforming Rosenhill bit by bit into a great big Villa Villekula, tirelessly working at making the world a little bit better.

Their grandparents started with producing apple juice from their own harvest and offered to extract must from apples of people in the surroundings in Rosenhill. Emilia and Lars joined the "Fruit Brokers".

For those who have apples to give away the exchange constitutes a platform to announce this, whilst people looking for apples will find any surplus there. Furthermore, anyone can learn how to make cider at Rosenhill.

The café and shop offers home-made cakes and seasonal snacks. Visitors will find quaint places to sit down everywhere on the farm. The owners' relaxed attitude and inexhaustible wealth of ideas are visible in every nook and cranny.

Next to the café is a large event space, adorned with colourful paper garlands. A small stage in a corner is flanked by a piano and a cat is sprawled out under an armchair.

In the summer months regular concerts and parties are held here that go on from the afternoon right into the wee hours. The ambience changes quite a bit then as young hip Stockholmers make for the rural idyll. For them Rosenhill is a trendy place to be. Those who like it a bit less loud can visit the "Give and Take Shop", participate in a yoga, percussion or felting class or amble across the flea market regularly taking place in the large car park. There is an abundance of options at all times.

Address Nyckelbyvägen 22, 17890 Stockholm-Ekerö, www.rosenhill-ekero.blogspot.com | **Public transport** Nyckelby (bus 309, 311, 312) | **Tip** Between May and September three small wooden huts offer the opportunity of staying overnight at Rosenhill. They sleep four and cost between 250 and 600 kronen, depending on the number of guests. A dip in Lake Mälar in the evening sun is an added bonus here.

74 Das »Rost« Stockholm
A place for everybody

An old motorcycle hangs above the entrance. Walking through it at first takes visitors to the café area, where the creative decoration continues. The counter and a small stage are made from steel parts left over when roofs in the area were renovated. Vintage American advertising signs adorn the walls, mainly promoting petrol and engine oil. A fuel pump incorporates a fully functional TV. Next to it stands a pinball machine. And a small flea market has been set up in a separate room.

The café is Zannah's empire. When the yoga teacher, who also works as an inspirational coach, opened the "Rost" together with her husband Staffan, the two realised their personal dream. The "Rost" wishes to be a meeting place – for people from the neighbourhood, artists and anyone who is open-minded and enjoys having a conversation with other people. The café has a piano and a guitar – anyone with a modicum of musical talent is invited to give a little performance.

It's not rare for neighbours popping in for a coffee to play a few pieces. When Zannah is not pampering her guests with various "Rost" sandwiches such as a "Rost Monsieur" or a "Rost 'n' Roll", her waffles or salads, she's probably busy in one of the back rooms. There she and a colleague give classes in yoga, including laughter yoga. Next door a guitar maker has opened up his workshop.

Between café and yoga room a pretty mullioned door hides Staffan's empire: a motorbike self-help workshop that runs counter to all clichés. Everything sparkles and shines here – a paradise for amateur wrench-wielders.

Bikers have the opportunity to work on their machines at eight spick-and-span workstations and talk shop with a cool drink, while loud laughter can be heard in the background and a café guest might be playing a few bars on the guitar.

Address Wollmar Yxkullsgatan 52, 11850 Stockholm-Södermalm | Public transport
Mariatorget (T-bana 13, 14) | Opening times Mon–Fri 11am–6pm, Sat and Sun
11am–5pm | Tip The "Snooker" in Krukmakargatan 34a has nine snooker tables, five
billiards tables and darts. It is Sweden's only snooker club.

75__Saltsjöbadens Friluftsbad

Back to 1920s summers

On his travels through Europe banker Knut Agathon Wallenberg realised that there was good money to be made from resorts and spa towns. This inspired him to buy a large swathe of farm land on the Baltic Sea in 1891 and, together with a few other investors, set up the summer and winter sports resort "Saltsjöbaden". Two elegant hotels and a sanatorium, as well as baths, a marina, a ski jump and toboggan runs were constructed. Wallenberg also had a rail connection to Stockholm built. Today, thanks to the commitment and hard work of a citizens' initiative, Saltsjöbaden's Friluftsbad is resplendent again in its original state, giving an idea of the glamour of bygone times.

The friendly bath house for ladies painted green and white (built in 1895) impresses with its unpretentious elegance, representative of the style of the time. On the large summer terrace visitors feel as if they had travelled back in time to the early 20th century. From here ladies may either step into the sea via two steps or jump into the cool waters from a diving board.

Wallenberg's original dream was of sumptuous baths in the Greek style including an amphitheatre. However, there wasn't quite enough money for that. Architect Torben Grut, who also designed the Olympic stadium, helped him fulfil at least part of his dream with the bathing house for men (1925).

Aesthetically completely different compared to the bathing house for women, this one took inspiration from a neoclassical temple. The creamy white building is surrounded by a bright red railing, with the wall on the terrace painted a strong blue. Between the two houses, where the amphitheatre was once supposed to be situated, a small bay with a sandy beach is enjoyed mainly by families with small children. They splash around happily and enjoy a trip in the spirit of a 1920s summer.

Address Torben Gruts väg 8, 13335 Stockholm-Saltsjöbaden | **Public transport** Saltsjöbaden (commuter train) | **Opening times** May–Aug 9am–6pm | **Tip** Right by the Saltjöduvnäs train station the former station building houses the restaurant "Stazione", which offers pizza for the return trip at very reasonable prices.

76_ The Sculpture Park

Arty treasure hunt in Vastertorp

Stepping out of the T-bana-Station Västertorp and walking left down Störtloppsvägen, a small bronze sculpture stands at the side of the street between advertising hoardings and scurrying passengers.

It's called "Old Man with Goat", and not only because of the goat is actually a bit reminiscent of Picasso's work. This is the first of 21 sculptures forming Stockholm's largest open-air sculpture collection.

Most were created by local artists and represent Swedish Modernism between 1930 and 1950. However, there is also a bronze sculpture by British iconic artist Henry Moore.

What is unusual is the neighbourhood housing the sculpture park. Västertorp is one of those suburbs created after World War II, when Stockholm's city boundaries were bursting at the seams. The monotony of streets lined by modest identical three-storey residential houses is only broken by the odd modern high-rise peaking out.

A shopping mall was built at the centre of the suburb. The construction firm "Olsson & Rose Lund AB" created the buildings in the northern part of the area. Västertorp has to thank its director Fritz H Eriksson for its rich treasure of public art. In 1945, Eriksson founded the Hägerstensåsen cultural association, which sponsored 16 of the sculptures.

The artworks aren't always easy to spot; the first pieces of the collection in particular require a keen eye. Those sculptures are found across from the "Old Man with Goat" on Västertorpsplan. This is where, on the left-hand side after passing a gate to enter the Västertorpspark the next artworks can be viewed. So, this stroll of some 1.5 kilometres/under a mile is not only appealing to culture vultures, but also to keen treasure hunters.

Address Västertorpspark between T-bana station Västertorp and Hägerstenåsen, 12947 Stockholm-Hägersten | **Public transport** Västertorp (T-bana 14) | **Tip** www.stockholm.bostream.se has a map marking the location of each sculpture.

77__The Sea God

Commander over heavy seas and doldrums

Squatting amidst the hustle and bustle at Skeppsbrokajen he watches what goes on, grinning. This is where the ferry to Djurgården leaves from, but steamboats and international shipping traffic stop here too.

Passengers come and go. Sjöguden, the Sea God, determines whether travellers will be heaving due to heavy seas or whether the sea will be as calm as glass.

The compact sculpture by well-known Swedish artist Carl Milles, made from red granite, is a little reminiscent of a Sumo ringer or a sea monster. It's probably meant to represent Triton, the Greek God of the Seas and son of Poseidon.

He can be identified by the trumpet snail in his left hand. When he blows his Triton horn, as it's known, he can whip up the seas or calm them, just as he wishes. The resulting cacophony sounds so awful that even giants take flight.

Triton is often represented with a human torso and a fish-like lower part. Thus, in Milles' artwork his ample thighs are only sketched, ending in a fin.

The sculpture was made in 1913, during a phase when Milles was still heavily influenced by the monumental work of German sculptor Adolf von Hildebrand. Milles had lived in Munich for two years and got to know Hildebrand's art philosophy there. Hildebrand was an advocate of a clear formal language dispensing with superfluous details.

Milles had wanted to design a further nine sculptures for the quay, but that plan didn't materialise; Sjöguden remained alone. Which doesn't seem to bother him – possibly because of the pretty mermaid snuggling up to his shoulders. She too is holding a shell in her hand; possibly we are looking at a nymph, a kind of assistant to the Gods.

Address Skeppsbrokajen, across from the restaurant "Zum Franziskaner", Skeppsbron 44,
11130 Stockholm-Gamla stan | Public transport Slussen (T-bana 13, 14, 17, 18, 19);
Räntmästartrappan (buses 2, 43, 55, 76, 96, 191–195) | Tip The restaurant "Zum
Franziskaner" at number 44 is allegedly the oldest one in town, having been founded
by a Franciscan monk. The quality of the food is debatable but beer and furnishings make
a visit worthwhile.

78 The Silk Weaving Museum
Rise, decline and rebirth

The workshop with its large spinning looms seems as alive as if the workers had just gone off for their break. And that impression is not even that wrong. When the descendants of company founder Almgren reopened the factory in 1991 as a museum, they partially took up production again. After 20 years of inactivity! A silk fabric woven for Drottningholm Palace in 1995 had a pattern last used in 1893.

Almgren's silk weavers is the oldest in Northern Europe, offering a comprehensive idea of the manufacture of silk fabrics. Visitors learn how the yarn is fed through the loom grid with the help of weft bobbins and wound onto a warping frame afterwards, and how the jacquard technology using punch cards greatly accelerated and facilitated the weaving process. Almgren had smuggled the technology in from France, hiding the 24 component parts in cognac vats and fruit crates.

At the same time this place tells us something about the development of Stockholm – from a poor craftsmen's town to a flourishing industrial metropolis around 1900 to the administrative city it is today.

Knut August Almgren founded his concern in 1833 and was nominated purveyor to the court in 1844. In 1874 the production had its heyday, with 196 looms and 288 workers. One of the reasons for their success was the headscarves popular at the time, of which Almgren produced 98,000 in that year alone – the first industrially-produced "luxury item" for women.

As Almgren's workforce consisted mainly of women, the museum also yields interesting glimpses of the day-to-day life of the workers. The economic crisis of the 1930s led to a sharp decline in demand for the fine fabrics. After World War II the weaving mill produced nearly exclusively medal ribbons before finally closing its doors in 1974.

Address Repslagargatan 15, 11846 Stockholm-Södermalm | Public transport Slussen (T-bana 13, 14, 17, 18, 19) | Opening times July–mid-Aug Mon–Sat 11am–3pm, at other times Mon–Fri 10am–4pm, Sat 11am–3pm, guided tours: Mon, Wed, Sat, Sun 1pm | Tip "Drop Coffee" at Wollmar Yxkullsgatan 10 serves in-house roasted coffee prepared with small china filters.

79 __ The Sisters
The veil of love

A young father is playing with his small daughter at her feet. Next to them a dog lifts its leg. And a group of young people going in the direction of busy Götgatan passes them without paying them any heed.

The two ladies look down on the cheerful hustle and bustle with a gentle and friendly expression. Naked back to back right on Mosebacke torg, they don't seem to be ashamed of wearing nothing but their birthday suit. To the contrary. One of them is sprawled out, hands behind her head, emphasising her fine body. The other holds a jar in her arm, pouring water over both their backs. She too is freely showing off her physical charms.

Are they muses? Or goddesses of poetry? The location of the sculpture in front of the Södra Teater seems to suggest this. And indeed, artist Nils Sjögren was initially working on a sculpture of Venus, the Roman goddess of love and erotic desire. However, when he heard about the harrowing fate of two women he decided to create a monument to them and their love.

These two ladies have occupied one of Stockholm's most beautiful squares since 1945. However, only a few of the passers-by hurrying past them every day know their sad story.

The two women were lesbians. Out of desperation for having to keep their love secret in the society of that time, they drowned themselves in 1911 in Stockholm's Hammarby Sjö. To do this they tied their bodies together and weighed down the veils of their hats with stones.

In their memory the gay community puts a veil round their shoulders during the annual "Pride Festival".

In 2012 the "Spartacus Guide", a guidebook for gay men, crowned Sweden the world's most gay-friendly country. Maybe that's why the two women look so content.

Address Mosebacke torg, 11646 Stockholm-Södermalm | Public transport Slussen
(T-bana 12, 14, 17, 18, 19) | Tip The terrace of Mosebacke offers refreshments and
fabulous views across Stockholm, described by Strindberg in "The Red Room".

80__ The Skandia Theatre
Cinema as it used to be

In a way, the glory days of cinema live on here, an era when the films attracted masses of viewers and finely furbished halls showed a programme filling all evening with news bulletins, supporting film and main feature. Golden sculptures of Adam and Eve mark the right and left of the Skandia Theatre screen. When the golden gathered curtain between them rises, the audience catch a glimpse of paradise. At least that was the plan of Swedish star architect Gunnar Asplund, when he built the cinema in 1923 in the neoclassical style popular at the time.

Numerous lovingly executed details indicate that this is indeed a place dedicated to pleasure and the arts. On the stone reliefs in the foyer, beautiful naked muses shove grapes into their mouths whilst another curvy naked creature dances. Goddess Luna, harp in hand, is lasciviously sprawled on an old spherical microphone dangling from the screen room's ceiling. It goes without saying that the seats are covered in red velvet. The separate waiting areas for ladies and gentlemen may still be viewed in the corridor.

This beautiful place doesn't show the many brutal modifications it had to suffer until achieving listed status in 2000 and reopening in 2001, practically in its original state. Only the technology was adapted to the modern era. While digital projection has come in, the old projectors are still operational. Apart from the odd special showing, the film listings don't give in too much to nostalgia. "Batman" and "James Bond" are shown alongside contemporary comedies. Everything in the original version with Swedish subtitles by the way.

Those who like authenticity should reserve the royal box at the back, on the right hand side. While the sound is not as good as in the other rows, the romantic surroundings more than make up for that.

Address Drottninggatan 82, 11136 Stockholm-Norrmalm, www.sf.de | Public transport Hötorget (T-bana 17, 18, 19) | Tip Drottninggatan 88 marks the entrance to the "Central-bad", vintage art-nouveau baths built in 1904. The shaded pretty courtyard is a welcome opportunity to flee from the urban hustle and bustle.

81 The Skinnarviks Mountain

A rocky plateau in the heart of the city

Rising 53 metres/174 feet above sea level, the Skinnarviksberg forms Stockholm's highest natural elevation, and the mound offers fine views of the city. In itself that wouldn't be much to write home about, as other points around the city yield impressive views too. What is special here is that you do feel like standing on a high-altitude summit – right in the heart of the city!

Not even five minutes from busy Hornsgatan, the narrow Gamla Lundagatan snakes past a few small 18th-century wooden houses, painted red and yellow. These are the last remains of the old workers' quarter that once stood here. In the 17th century the mound was first settled by knackers and tanners. The eastern banks of the Södermälarstrand was called Skinnarvik at the time – the Bay of the Skinners.

There was plenty of the water they needed for their work here. Also they were far enough from the town centre at the time; tanning animal hides was a fairly smelly business. At a later stage, workers employed at textile factories, a brewery and other industries settled here.

In Gamla Lundagatan the urban noise lessens perceptibly, and the ambience is more reminiscent of a village. At its end a narrow path leads uphill, and suddenly you're standing on the summit. Only tree tops line the extensive rock plateau. The telegraph mast standing in its centre adds even more to the impression of standing on a mountain ridge. At the foot of the mountain lies glittering Lake Mälar, the sparkling spire of the Stadshuset is visible in the distance, and to the right is a view of Riddarholmen.

Which place could be better suited to a romantic tryst? Swedish singer Amanda Mair even dedicated a song to the Skinnarviksberg: "I have a bottle of wine and a blanket that I'd like to share with you … Upon the hill … you know the one …" Well, go ahead!

Address Skinnarviksberget, 11823 Stockholm-Södermalm | **Public transport** Zinkens-damm (T-bana 14) | Tip On Skinnarbacke, at the corner of Lundagatan, look for the "Skinnarvikskiosken". The small green wooden hut, decorated with curtains and geraniums, sells ice-cream, coffee and cake. Alongside the kiosk, a hammock and deck chairs beckon to rest tired feet.

82 The Skittle Alley

Skittling in style at Villa Camitzka

Warm sunlight streams into the long hall through the tall windows. The open truss gives the space a light and airy feeling. Skittle balls lie ready in a bowl and nine wooden pins wait at the end of the smooth wooden alley.

Where in modern skittle alleys the balls would disappear in a hole and be automatically transported back to the players, here the impact is cushioned by bales of straw.

In this 19th-century skittle alley the balls are rolled back by hand via a ramp on the side. At Villa Camitzka in the Torekällberget open-air museum one can not only admire this vintage skittle alley but play on it too.

In the 19th century the small port of Södertälje south of Stockholm was a very popular spa town, its climate enjoying an excellent reputation. In summer, rich guests from Stockholm and other towns would visit the spa and stroll through the adjacent park. Many holidaymakers actually owned a summer house in the area.

Originally, Villa Camitzka was situated close to the spa park and belonged to a rich mill owner. It was surrounded by extensive gardens where in summer much of the social life would take place. Lush flowers, some of them exotic, would blossom in all colours around the well-kept lawns. There were vegetable patches, fruit bushes and trees, as well as a tree house, which no garden could be without at that time.

The estate conveys a lively impression of the way wealthy Swedes would spend their summer holidays in the second half of the 19th century. During skittle breaks the ladies would stroll through the garden – in their long dresses presumably – whilst the gentlemen would partake of some high-proof spirits in the salon next door.

On cooler days the party would gather together in front of the fireplace.

Address Torekällberget, 15145 Stockholm-Södertälje, www.sodertalje.se/torekallberget |
Public transport Södertälje centrum (commuter train); Torekällberget (bus 751) | Opening
times June–Aug daily 10am–6pm, at other times 10am–4pm | Tip The open-air museum
offers a visit to various town and rural houses providing a glimpse of life in the 19th and
early 20th century. One of them, a general store, is particularly worth seeing.

83 __ The Skogs Chapel
Solace in nature

Standing amidst dense conifer trees, the forest chapel by the great Swedish architect Gunnar Asplund first appears like a modest cottage. The only ornament is the golden Angel of Death by Carl Milles on the wood shingle roof above the entrance. The angel receives visitors with open arms. The chapel, inaugurated in 1920, is the first and smallest on Stockholm's large forest cemetery. The Danish pleasure palace of Liselund, the world's only thatched palace, had inspired Asplund to design this building.

In 1915, Asplund and Sigurd Lewerentz, who had met at university, won the competition for designing the forest cemetery. The concept developed by the two architects placed humankind at the centre – the visitors of the cemetery, the mourners with their feelings. The architects wanted them to find solace in nature, symbolising the cycle of life, and thus be accompanied in their pain.

As a consequence, the small forest chapel is surrounded by a low stone wall inside which the trees are noticeably denser. They are intended to give the mourners the opportunity to collect their thoughts before taking their leave of the departed. Inside visitors are greeted by a surprisingly light-filled room with a pantheon-like dome which conveys a feeling of lightness. After the ceremony the mourners are led out through another entrance into a bright open landscape intended to make their return to life easier. Impressively designed through and through the chapel is full of fascinating details. The key-hole at the entrance represents the eye of a death's head and the cast-iron gate bears a host of Christian symbols.

Asplund and Lewerentz, who were behind this impressive landscaping, completed the cemetery in 1940. Gunnar Asplund was to die only a few months after its inauguration. On the plain stone marking his grave in front of the Chapel of Faith is the inscription: "His Work Lives On".

Address Sockenvägen 492, 12233 Stockholm-Enskede | **Public transport** Skogskyrkogården (T-bana 18; bus 161) | **Opening times** Visitors Center 25 May–7 Sept daily 11am–5pm, guided tours in English: Sun 10.30am, tel. +468/50831659 | **Tip** The former children's cemetery near the forest chapel is an emotional place; a few of the gravestones are still standing. Deciduous trees instead of conifers lend the site a lighter character. The area lies in a depression in the ground, creating a feeling of calm security.

84__ Slussen

A rather underestimated place

Most people only know Slussen as an ugly transit hub, whose dilapidated corridors are best avoided. Still, without this place Stockholm would not be the flourishing city it is today.

The lock connects Lake Mälar with the Baltic Sea, fresh water with salt water. It wasn't always thus. A lock became necessary because of the city's founder Birger Jarl. Until the mid-13th century Lake Mälar was a bay of the Baltic Sea with slightly salty water. Birger Jarl had the daring idea to erect a dam and seal off the fjord from the Baltic Sea. The regent's drastic measure served to protect Stockholm and the hinterland from attacks. It also interrupted an important trading route. From then on all goods had to be transported overland from the ports on the Lake Mälar side to the Baltic Sea side. This promoted Stockholm development into a flourishing trade city and in time the ecosystem of Lake Mälar converted to freshwater.

The first lock creating a new link between the Baltic Sea and Lake Mälar dates from 1642. In 1935 the cloverleaf interchange was built with road, water and rail traffic spread over several levels.

At the time Slussen was a very modern, elegant place. Large shiny glass fronts sheltered fancy shops and chic cafés. This was the spot of the city's first water closet. People would come from far away only to visit the Slussen toilet. At Christmas time the Slussen terrace was adorned by a splendid Christmas tree and in summertime by a Midsummer pole. As time went on, maintenance and upkeep of the facility became too costly and Slussen increasingly deteriorated.

For years, renovation was deemed to be impossible. Since the 1990s several calls for proposals were issued for architects to submit a master plan with the aim of letting Slussen shine in a new light. Currently, rebuilding work is scheduled to be completed by 2020.

Address Slussen, 11645 Stockholm-Södermalm | Public transport Slussen (commuter train and T-bana 13, 14, 17, 18, 19) | Tip Some scenes for the movie "The Girl with the Dragon Tattoo" starring Daniel Craig were filmed in the "Gula Gången", or "yellow corridor" underground passage.

85 __ The Sports Museum

A museum for tactile participation

The so-called sports laboratory in the basement of the Riksidrotts-museet offers an eminently practical access to "sports". That small red apparatus for instance serves to measure the muscle power of the hand and lower arm. For this, one has to press together the handle of the device with a bit of force, which leaves many a visitor red in the face. The result appears on a display. If visitors remain unhappy with the outcome despite all efforts and after repeated attempts, a sign recommends they train their muscles on the climbing wall around the   corner.

Another station comprises two starting blocks and a short run-ning track for visitors to test their reactions. A bit further on they can judge how developed their sense of balance is. The challenge is to walk backwards across a balance beam with a small bag of peas on your head. Depending on who happens to be wobbling across the beam at the time of your visit the performance can end up quite en-tertaining.

The theoretical departments of the sports museum are very origi-nally designed and well worth a visit. The permanent exhibition on the first floor informs on the beginnings of Swedish sports, the rela-tionship between sports and politics and the history of female ath-letes, who for a long time had to fight discrimination. Visitors can find out when the first sports clubs for working men were founded and why in Sweden it's mainly rural associations who are successful in football and bandy. It goes without saying that the father of Swedish gymnastics, Pehr Henrik Ling is mentioned too.

Possibly the most entertaining items are black-and-white photo-graphs of neatly dressed secretaries sitting behind their typewriter twisting their arms into gymnastic poses. A collection of historic sports dress, containing a skate that looks absolutely antique are also exhibited.

Address Djurgårdsbrunnsvägen 26, 11527 Stockholm-Djurgården | Public transport Sjöhistoriska museet (bus 69) | Opening times Mon–Fri 12 noon–5pm, Sat and Sun 11am–5pm | Tip An old house on the eastern side of the nearby small peninsula Hundudden is believed to be from 1697. Used to store gunpowder under King Karl XI, it is used as a café today: "Kafé Krudhus" (Wed–Sun 10am–5pm).

86 St Mark's Church

The perfection of the seemingly imperfect

The rough facade of St Mark's Church forms an impressive contrast to the smooth functionalist buildings surrounding it. Constructed in 1963, the low building appears like a bulwark against the anonymity and uniformity of modern times. To the same extent that no one human being resembles the next, a special firing technique ensured that no stone resembled the other here.

In the mid-1950s the parish and the city were planning a new church in the recent suburb of Björkhagen, suitable for both spiritual and secular meetings. The chosen spot was a drained swamp occupying a central location on the T-bana station and adorned by a pretty birch copse. The selection committee decided on the design by Swedish architect Sigurd Lewerentz, 70 at the time, whose perfectionism was legendary. True enough, with St Markus Church he lived up to his reputation once again.

Whilst the brutalist style of architecture doesn't readily disclose it, everything has been planned to the last detail. This is the perfection of the not-quite perfect. On a daily basis Lewerentz would discuss progress with the local craftsmen, asking them to change their usual way of working a little. What Lewerentz wanted to avoid was the straight and standardised look.

From the benches covered with their sheep pelts for kneeling churchgoers down to the brass psalm numbers suspended from simple nails Lewerentz designed everything himself.

Never losing sight of the human dimension, he created a beautifully tiled anteroom next to the church nave where brides-to-be could prepare for the ceremony and check their look in the mirror one last time. Through the way he placed altar and pulpit Lewerentz even deliberately influenced the sequence of the services. The fact that the pastor has to cover a little distance first creates a break before the sermon.

Address Malmövägen 51, 12149 Stockholm-Johanneshov | Public transport Björkhagen (T-bana 17) | Opening times Mon–Fri 9am–4pm | Tip Built in 1956 by Hungarian architect Georg Varhelyi, the 16-storey high-rise on Björkhagsplan 1–9 was for a long time considered Sweden's highest residential building.

87 __ Stigbergets Borgarrum

The legacy of an impressive woman

The Fjällgatan on Södermalm is well-known for its unique views of Djurgården and the city centre. Pretty little 18th-century houses stand here too. They are inhabited and not open for visitors.

The former flat of the Social-Democrat politician and women's rights activist Anna Lindhagen (1870–1941) forms an exception to the rule.

Lindhagen was one of the early 20th-century pioneers of a movement dedicated to the conservation of old buildings, even if, as in the case of Södermalm, they weren't palaces or stately homes.

However, this was only one of the fields that Anna Lindhagen was active in. A nurse by training, she was the first to campaign for state support for widows and fatherless children. She was also active in the women's movement and is considered the founder of the Swedish allotment gardens movement (see page 16). Between 1911 and 1923 she was the only woman to hold a seat for the Social Democrats in Stockholm's city government and also a member of the city's Urban Beautification Council.

In the 1920s and 1930s Anna Lindhagen was one of the best-known personalities on Södermalm. At first she only lived in two rooms on Fjällgatan 34. The remaining four rooms were inhabited by a captain. When the captain moved out in 1929, Lindhagen took over those rooms too.

Furnishing the flat with pieces from the mid-19th century she made it accessible to the public as a museum. Some of the items one can admire in the lovingly looked-after rooms with the creaking floorboards are an original 19th-century kitchen and a charming dollhouse. Lindhagen also put on salon evenings in the museum space, inviting famous personalities from arts and politics.

Today still the occasional readings and talks take place. It's also possible to rent the flat for private parties.

STIGBERGETS
BORGARRUM

←

Address Fjällgatan 34, 11628 Stockholm-Södermalm | Public transport Ersta sjukhus
(bus 2, 53, 96) | Opening times 15 Jan–31 May and Sept–15 Dec Sun 1–3pm | Tip The
artwork opposite the house with the number 32 commemorates Anna Lindhagen. It is
made to look like a large coin, with a portrait of the dynamic politician on the obverse.

88_ The Stora Blecktorn Park

Anything a child could wish for

Sheep and goats in the heart of the city? That and much more is on offer in the extensive Blecktorn Park, a paradise for children. The large playground with its picturesque backdrop is only a five-minute walk from the T-bana station Skanstull.

Blecktorn Park's biggest attraction are the animals. It all started in 1989 with a ram; since then the number of animals has increased significantly. Today, a Canadian mini pig, two guinea pigs, two rabbits, two African dwarf goats and three sheep live here. The roofs of modern urban buildings jut up behind the even-toed ungulates peacefully grazing next to the playground, creating a futuristic ambience.

On the playground children have the opportunity to gain a glimpse of the rural world of animal husbandry. Every day at 9.30am and 4pm they can be present when Tulle the pig is fed. Educators offer one-hour classes for children between six and ten years of age who want to learn more about the animals and their care. After that the little ones may feed the animals themselves and participate in a "rabbit jump".

Part of the playground is a public preschool which – as is the case with all activities on the facility – is run by trained educators employed by the city of Stockholm. Every day groups sing, craft something, play or read a story. Of course kids can use the slides and swings, climb and seesaw. On weekends there are regular barbecues, on Thursday afternoons they can have their face painted, and on Friday afternoons, waffles with cream are served.

In winter, when the ground is covered with snow, Blecktorn Park offers special fun for all ages, as the slopes then turn into wonderful sled runs.

Address Between Tullgårdsgatan and Blecktornsstigen, 11668 Stockholm-Södermalm | Public transport Skanstull (T-bana 17, 18, 19); Nätgränd (bus 55) | Opening times Mon–Thu 9.15am–5.15pm, Fri 9.15am–5pm, Sat (April–Sept only) and Sun 11am–4pm | Tip The building with the towers on Södermannagatan 61 gave the park its name: Stora Blecktornet. From 1930 to 1935 this was the residence of architect Ferdinand Boberg. The building now houses a public café, run, among others, with the help of people with learning disabilities.

89 The Storken Pharmacy
Sweden's most beautiful dispensary

Back in antiquity, the serpent was taken as a symbol of the art of healing. Here, rather than coiled around the Aesculapian staff it is shown inside the beak of a stork. The golden bird enjoys pride of place above the entrance to the Storken Pharmacy, putting visitors in the mood for its opulent interior.

The preserved original furnishings made from noble polished rosewood, ebony and jacaranda date back to 1899 and give the place a near-sacral appearance. Portraits lining the intricately carved shelves in the neo-Gothic style immortalise Swedish doctors and scientists: Jöns Jakob Berzelius for instance, who introduced a system of symbols for chemical elements. Depending on their level of fame, the researchers are commemorated with a small medallion or an impressive golden bust. Below them, 100 year old pharmacist's jars with Latin inscriptions stand next to discreet modern products. The walls are made of Swedish marble, the ceiling of painted stained glass by German artist Fritz Rosenthal. They show allegorical representations of illness and good health, life and death: a sick man is writhing in the arms of a woman, while the Grim Reaper is waiting in the background.

Small wonder that the Swedish conservation authorities listed this pharmacy as the one with the greatest cultural and historical significance in the country. Apart from the brown glass apothecary bottles the back room preserves further instruments in their original state, but most of all jars with a rather peculiar content. There is a small bowl with dried green iridescent flies. Contrary to popular belief the Spanish Fly was not an invention of the sex industry, as one can find out here. Ground to a powder in a mortar the insect works as an potency enhancer. Overdosed, the Spanish Fly leads to circulatory collapse and renal failure, leading to its use in the past for executions or secret assassinations.

Address Storgatan 28, 11455 Stockholm-Östermalm | **Public transport** Karlaplan (T-bana 13), Östermalmstorg (T-bana 13, 14) | **Opening times** Mon–Fri 9am–6pm | **Tip** Inside the house, one of the first the first electric lifts in Sweden dates back to the late 19th century and is particularly well preserved.

90 __ The Storkyrkobad

Baths in the true sense of the word

Lying hidden in a backyard in the heart of the Gamla stan historic district and belonging to a primary school, the Storkyrkobad is situated in an 18th-century cellar vault below the school building. In the daytime kids yell, practice front crawl or train for the swimming certificate.

When evening comes, the small pool opens its doors to the public. At that point the pace slows down as the guests swim the lanes in subdued light sometimes even by candlelight and classical music.

The property upon which the school is located can look back on a long history. In the Middle Ages there was a Dominican monastery here and in the 17th century the well-known court painter David Klocker Ehrenstrahl built a stately villa.

In the 18th century the municipal cellar master Peter Hinrich Fuhrmann moved into the villa with his wife Margarete Götze. The royal wine purveyor converted the subterranean vault into a wine and coal cellar. The cast-iron ornamentation with the initials PHFMG above the entrance to the courtyard is a reminder of that era.

One particularity are the baths' shower rooms. Six small porcelain tubs stand one beside the other below the shower heads; they once served to bathe the children.

As early as the 19th century, when the Storkyrkoskola moved into the building, small tin tubs were set up in the cellar, as few families had access to their own bathroom at the time. When the school was extensively refurbished in 1932, a pool was built that included changing rooms and showers in the cellar. The tin tubs were then replaced with porcelain ones.

Of course it is possible to take a regular shower here. On the other hand, there are adults who prefer a hip bath in small tubs, chatting away with their neighbour.

Address Svartmangatan 20–22, 11129 Stockholm-Gamla stan | Public transport Gamla stan (T-bana 13, 14, 17, 18, 19) | Opening times During term time: 5pm–8.30pm, Men's Day: Tue, Fri and Sun, Women's Day: Mon and Thu | Tip The Storkyrkobad offers a candle-lit massage on a lounge at the rim of the pool (for reservations call: tel. +468/209027).

91_ The Sun Boat
A very special eye

Is this the abstract representation of an ear? Or a boxing glove with a hole? You can read a lot into the sculpture by Swedish sculptor Christian Berg. The artist himself called it Sun Boat, reporting that a stay in the Greek Aegean had inspired him to this work. With a little imagination the bright curved form standing on a granite block can be taken for a billowing sail.

Since 1966 the artwork has occupied its place on the Evert Taubes Terrass, offering one of the finest views of the city. No matter what one sees in the sculpture, its most important feature is the oval opening in the centre.

Depending on which step of the terrace people stand on, it will always frame something different, even if it's only a particularly pretty cloud. In this way it lends the already charming view an additional dimension.

Stretching out behind the sculpture, the Riddarfjärden is spanned in the distance by the impressive arches of the Väster Bridge. To the right is the shining golden dome of the Stadshus, to the left Södermalm with the former brewery. The best time to be here is an early summer's evening when the tourist buses negotiating the cobblestones have left and the last civil servants have left their offices in the surrounding court and administrative buildings. Then the streets between the old palaces of the Riddarholmen nobility are quiet.

The place takes its name from the famous Swedish singer and composer Evert Taube, who enjoyed an ecstatic reception from the audience in the Grönalund leisure park. Since 1980 he has been commemorated by a small bronze sculpture on the northern side of the terrace.

But even the musician lets his lute rest, pointing instead in admiration at the views.

Address Evert Taubes Terrass, 11128 Stockholm-Gamla stan | **Public transport** Gamla stan (T-bana 13, 14, 17, 18, 19) | **Tip** The small kiosk on the terrace sells drinks and snacks and the handful of tables and chairs in front invite you to sit down. The kiosk remains open for as long as there are customers.

92 The Supreme Court's Roof

Get that Karlsson-on-the-Roof feeling

Visitors are not allowed up here on their own, as the former parliamentary building now houses the Supreme Court. However, the "Upplev mer" operator offers an experience they call Roof Walks.

The guide welcomes groups in front of the house, accompanying them to an elevator that is imbued in as much history as everything else on Riddarholmen. At the top, a steep set of stairs awaits, leading up to the court building's roof timbering. Straw spills out from between old wooden beams. This is where visitors are issued helmets and climbing harnesses – the same equipment that is used to protect workers on Norwegian oil platforms. Well, that's reassuring …

A steep set of stairs finally leads onto the roof. All of a sudden everything else seems unimportant and even the fact that everyone looks pretty silly in their safety harnesses plays no role whatsoever. The views are breathtakingly beautiful. On one side Lake Mälaren glitters in the evening sun, on the other the Baltic Sea stretches out. From up here one can see the golden tip of the Stadshuset, the old brewery on Södermalm, the royal palace and the Nicolai Church. Somehow it wouldn't be surprising if all of a sudden a small fat man with a propeller on his back stepped out from behind a chimney. Astrid Lindgren's famous Karlsson automatically comes to mind.

But after all this is a walk and so the tour goes on once around the entire roof. Despite the sophisticated safety gear a queasy thrill remains. The guided tour also takes visitors on a trip back in time, which distracts from thinking too much about being this high up. It is more about the old Vikings, former execution sites and bloody wars. So once harness and helmet have been taken off and the group is safe and sound back on the ground again one is glad somehow to have returned back to the here and now.

Address Birger Jarls torg 5, 11128 Stockholm-Riddarholmen, www.upplevmer.se | Public transport Gamla stan (T 13, 14, 17, 18, 19); Riddarhustorget (bus 3, 53) | Opening times To make a reservation call tel. +468/223005 or book through the homepage; guided tours are available in English too | Tip In the neighbouring alley, Schering Rosenhanes gränd, the wall of a house has been built around a rock featuring a black iron flap. This hides the first Swedish altitude measuring system dating back to 1886 upon which all maps at the time were based.

93_ Svenska Hem
Made by women for women

In the chic fashion boutique, only the antique glass ceiling with the golden stars remind of bygone days. It was here that a small revolution took place in the early 20th century. The place housed a branch of what was then known as a "Svenska Hem", a shop selling quality food and household goods run by women, where only women were allowed to shop.

At the time, quality standards for food weren't very high. Anna Whitlock, head of a Stockholm school, had seen a few pupils die of cholera and wanted to do something about that. During a trip to England she sought advice from English women's rights activists and representatives of trade cooperatives, all in the hands of men.

After her return Whitlock founded her own cooperative with a few like-minded women. For the equivalent of some two euros women were able to purchase a minimum share and place their orders in pretty shops comfortably seated on a stool. They were also able to borrow household appliances, take classes and familiarise themselves with new technical equipment.

"Svenska Hem" published the first consumer's newspaper with recipes and technical tips, explaining for instance how to repair a vacuum cleaner.

The male traders took exception to the point of getting Swedish suppliers to boycott "Svenska Hem". Only cooperatives in Rotterdam and London continued to deliver merchandise.

Still, that proved to be sufficient, business was booming. At the height of their success Stockholm had five branches stocking some 4,000 items.

Eventually though the company suffered in World War I, having to join forces with the smaller "Consumers' Association Stockholm". A few years later there was no shop under female management left.

Address Jakobsbergsgatan 6, 11144 Stockholm-Norrmalm | Public transport Östermalms-torg (T-bana 13, 14) | Tip At Kungsgatan 3, the "Svenskt Snus" shop sells snuff tobacco from all over the world. In the tastefully furnished shop, which serves coffee too, visitors can learn everything about snuff, the famous Snus.

94 Sweden's longest escalator

The discovery of slowness

Up until the mid-1960s Västraskogen was a hilly suburb with a large forested area and a handful of single or multi-family homes. Then the Solna municipality cleared the western woods, erecting tenement blocks and office towers in their stead. At first glance Västraskogen doesn't seem to be a very special kind of place. However, first impressions are deceiving here.

Västraskogen Tunnelbana station, built in 1975 to link up this neighbourhood with the city centre, offers a very special experience: riding Sweden's longest escalator. With a length of 66 metres/216 feet, it covers a height difference of 33 metres/108 feet. Speed is a gentle 0.75 metres/2.5 feet per second, making one trip last around one-and-a-half minutes. The feeling passengers get during the trip is the exact opposite of a speed rush; this smooth gliding movement brings about more of a pleasant calm, approaching a near-meditative state.

On the naked rock walls to the right and left no modern advertising hoardings distract from the experience. At the foot of the steps the rock gives way to colourful tiles which don't interfere with the calm ambience.

Fellow citizens in a hurry who like to dash down the escalators give up after a few steps. The flight of stairs is simply too long, the steps too high, the whole thing too tiring.

For decades, the escalator of Västraskogen was even considered to be the longest one in Western Europe. But the way it is with records, the day comes when it's time to vacate the position. As happened in 2003 when a new escalator in a Frankfurt shopping centre pushed Västraskogen off its throne. On the other hand, what is gliding in a crammed shopping mall against experiencing the calm of Västraskogen?

Address Västra Skogen T-bana, 17161 Stockholm-Solna | Public transport Västraskogen (T-bana 10, 11; bus 113, 196, 507) | Tip The square outside the station features an original artwork by Roland Persson. "Land of Plenty" (2001) comprises colourful cushions that look light as feather, but were made of cast bronze and then given a coat of varnish. The sculpture is supposed to lend the cold anonymous place a little cosy vibe.

95__ The Tanto Colony
Blooming gardens out of an emergency

The rocky mound rising up amidst the extensive Tantolunden park drops down on one side towards Årstaviken Bay. The hill is dotted with many small colourful wooden sheds surrounded by lush flourishing gardens. Though situated in the heart of Södermalm, heavenly peace reigns here – not to be confused with idleness: there is plenty of digging, planting and harvesting going on in these gardens.

In contrast to other allotment colonies this one initially served an eminently practical purpose. The first plots of land in Tantolunden were distributed by the city during WWI when food was scarce. Citizens were supposed to grow potatoes and other vegetables there. The rule is valid to this day. Those renting a plot commit themselves to using the major part of the soil to grow vegetables.

After the end of the war the gardens were appreciated more for their leisure value. The first small wooden garden sheds were erected on the plots in the 1920s. The designs by the well-known architects Ragnar Östberg and Lars Israel Wahlman were particularly popular. Some of them may be admired to this day. Between the two world wars however many colonies were torn down. The city grew and land was in short supply. The plots in Tantolunden were earmarked to make way for a hospital.

Then World War II came and the fruit and vegetables voluntarily cultivated by the local allotment gardeners contributed in no little way to alleviating the population's hunger. And when living space got scarce, many a garden shed was converted into long-term accommodation.

In the 1960s the colony was again threatened by demolition. Today nobody mentions this anymore. A stroll through the Tanto Colony is a popular pastime. People are proud of the well-kept gardens and the old-fashioned garden sheds. Two of the houses even made it to the Skansen open-air museum on Djurgården.

Address Tantolunden, 11734 Stockholm-Södermalm | **Public transport** Hornstull
(T-bana 13, 14; bus 40, 77, 94, 151, 191, 192, 726, 743, 745) | **Tip** Why not play a round
of minigolf at Tantogårdens's Bangolfklubb?

96__ The Tea House
A charming place of calm

Hidden behind trees and shrubs, the "Zui-Ki-Tei" tea house is located on a small mound next to the ethnographic museum. It might not appear that way but the location as well as every other detail has been subject to meticulous consideration.

A winding sandy path lined by small natural stones leads to a simple wooden gate. Visitors should stop at the first stone and start letting go of day-to-day life. And indeed the charming calm of the tea house already makes itself felt from this point. The tea house was constructed using raw natural materials such as pine and cedar wood as well as bamboo.

The shrubs, trees and mosses in the garden are deliberately kept in subdued colours, creating a gentle ambience. The house follows the Wabi Sabi concept of tea master and Zen monk Sen-no-Rikyu. This philosophy values hidden beauty over an obvious flawless one. Seen in this perspective, beauty is something which is inconspicuous or might even have small flaws.

Water splashes over a rock in front of the house. Once more visitors pause and prepare themselves for the tea ceremony by washing their hands and rinsing their mouthes. Inside the house they cross a narrow corridor to reach the large tea room. At weekends it's possible to participate in a public tea ceremony. The small room next door is exclusively reserved for "professionals". The goal of a tea ceremony is inner calm and inner balance. To become a master requires arduous and intensive training.

Inside the tea room the principle of Sen-no-Rikyu reappears. The flowers in a vase have subtle colours, and a full moon with clouds is carved into the wall. According to the Zen monk, the truly beautiful is not the bright glare of the sun, but the mild shining of the moon.

Address Djurgårdsbrunnsvägen 34, 11527 Stockholm-Djurgården | **Public transport** Museiparken (bus 69E) | **Opening times** Guided tours: 3 July – 28 Aug Wed 1pm or by appointment; tea ceremonies take place at weekends; to register call tel. +4610/4561299 or visning@etnografiskamuseet.se | **Tip** Beginners' classes for anyone interested in learning how to conduct Japanese tea ceremonies are offered twice a year at the Japanese Society (www.valrdskulturmuseerna.se, under Calendar).

97__The Tegnérlundenpark
Where thoughts take wings

In truth it's only a lightly curved green space amidst tall houses built at the turn of the past century and crisscrossed by a few trails. However, it is during dusk that this place develops a particular charm. Then one can imagine how Astrid Lindgren on her way home to the Vasa neighbourhood saw a young boy sitting on a bench. That got her thinking ... He might be living in one of the nearby houses? And she asked herself why he preferred to sit here in the dark instead of going home.

As she carried on musing about this she had the idea of a genie-in-a-bottle taking the boy with it into a faraway land. That was the birth of the idea for her book "Mio, My Son".

In Tegnérlunden Park, a bronze sculpture of the famous children's author commemorates the fact that this place inspired many of her stories. Sitting on the bench in front of the Lindgren sculpture, you can spot a mound supporting a small pavilion. This is where a spring comes up, its waters running through a brook and into a pond at the foot of the hill. Sitting on the shoulders of the author is Mister Lilyvale, who every evening takes the sick boy Goran with him into the land of twilight. A country where everything is possible, where young boys can drive trams and fly over church steeples. The popular author has opened her coat to warm and protect a boy crouching in the foreground, his eyes closed. Could it be that he's listening to one of her stories?

Once dusk falls Tegnérlunden Park lies deserted, with the lights being switched on in the surrounding houses. Is this Goran looking out of the window? And isn't that the tiny Mister Lilyvale perched on the window sill? Was that sound a car passing or was it Karlsson's propeller? In this place and with Astrid Lindgren behind you thoughts start flying. And anything is possible in the twilight hours.

Address Tegnérlunden, 11359 Stockholm-Norrmalm | Public transport Rådmansgatan (T-bana 17, 18, 19); Tegnérgatan (bus 65) | Tip For decades, Astrid Lindgren lived nearby, at Dalagatan 46. At www.astridlindgren.se one can take a virtual tour of the author's flat.

98__ Tellus
Back to the Eighties

Visiting "Tellus" is taking a small trip back in time, back to the 1980s. Four ladies between 30 and 60 years of age are seated around one of the black varnished wooden tables. Each has a robust ceramic tea mug in front of her. In one hand they hold crochet and knitting needles. For five years the knitting and crochet group has been meeting up at Tellus every second Thursday.

This is less about the consultation and exchange of knitting patterns – they're all professionals here after all – but about the personal exchange of ideas.

All it needs to prove that the group is very productive is a look at the surrounding tables that are full of an impressive selection of crocheted covers in bright colours.

When the small 1920s cinema was threatened with closure in 1986, a citizens' initiative was formed. This in turn led to an association, which today counts over 70 members. They run this unusual arts centre on a voluntary basis. Three times a week current films are shown. The in-house café hosts regularly changing arts exhibitions as well as music events. Not to mention the language circles and working groups on various topics. In one corner there is a small shelf with the label: "Take a book, give a book." The project is financed by admission fees, the Friends of Tellus association and the city of Stockholm.

The spirit of the 1980s remains alive to this day. Indeed the furnishings seem a little retro and the ambience is a little reminiscent of the tea rooms en vogue at the time. Everyone is welcome and encouraged to give free rein to their artistic side. While the Tellus can't be hired for private events, anyone wishing to mount an exhibition or give a concert may suggest this to the association. The decisions are taken democratically during the monthly meetings. Needless to say with all 70 members!

Address Vattenledningsvägen 46, 12633 Stockholm-Hägersten, www.tellusbio.nu | Public transport Midsommarkransen (T-bana 14) | Opening times The café usually opens one hour before the film starts; check the schedule online. | Tip Every two weeks there's after-work jazz at the Tellus between 5 and 6.30pm. The excellent in-house band performs, welcoming the occasional guest musician.

99__ The Temporära Konsthallen

Movement in arts

Choreographer Anna Asplind and art historian Linda Karlsson have been friends since the age of five. Actually, it was aged five that Linda was already running her first art gallery in the cellar of her parents' house. The inspiration for the "Temporära Konsthallen" and the two women's first shared gallery project came from Germany.

When Anna returned home after spending four years in Berlin the Stockholm art scene seemed fairly static and closed to her by comparison. She told Linda about her experiences in Berlin and the two friends decided to open up new art locations in Stockholm.

Before the two were able to convince the city to let them use the Danvikens Hospital for this purpose, the former institution for mental patients had been standing empty for decades. This had left its marks on the 18th-century building. The ground floor boasts a large light-filled hall with wooden flooring and a high ceiling whereas the room next door is only covered with gravel. Everywhere there are a raw brick walls or views toward the roof structure through holes in the open ceilings. The first floor generally lacks any kind of flooring. Visitors cross the former patients' rooms on an improvised wooden walkway. Exhibitions are usually held on the lower floors, with the artists often using the space as an integral part of their artwork and inspiration.

The first artists were hand-picked by Anna and Linda, the next ones came through recommendation from other artists and so it continued. That's exactly the way the young gallerists like it – open and flexible. It's not certain for how long the Temporära Konsthallen can stay in the former hospital, but the two friends are not worried. Stockholm has plenty more empty buildings only waiting to be discovered and filled with life.

Address Sjökvarnsbacken, 13171 Nacka, visit www.temporarakonsthallen.nu for information on exhibitions and the current location of the Temporära Konsthallen | Tip The "Färgfabrik" is another interesting art location. The former paint factory features exhibitions focussing on art and architecture, ateliers, workshops, concerts and parties (www.fargfabriken.se).

100__The Tensta Konsthall

Art overcomes boundaries

In the 1960s, the goal of the Swedish government's "Millions Programme" was to erect a million modern flats within the decade. This did indeed happen, mainly because emphasis was more on fast execution than on design.

Initially, the new prefab buildings were greeted enthusiastically, the flats were considered relatively spacious and comfortable. In 1969 the first tenants moved into Tensta, many families with small children amongst them.

Today, Tensta is a multicultural neighbourhood. Of the 17,000 people living here, two thirds are immigrants. Nearly half of Tensta's residents are out of work, many depend on social security. The fact that the "Tensta Konsthall" was founded here of all places, in the heart of what is considered a problematic neighbourhood, actually forms part of its concept. With its exhibitions, the museum puts a focus on cultural variety, aiming to promote dialogue between the cultures. Underpinning this is the conviction that exhibitions help convey the idea of art and culture and thus have a positive impact on social cohesion.

Since its foundation in 1998 Tensta Konsthall has risen to be an internationally recognised centre for contemporary art. Two or three exhibitions generally are held simultaneously.

The museum cooperates directly with artists and takes an active part in the genesis of their artworks, such as in the Projekt 16304, which was shown at the Venice Biennale and New York's New Museum.

Moreover, the Tensta Konsthall offers a comprehensive educational programme, developing projects for children and adolescents together with schools, often with the collaboration of artists. The Konsthall also offers plenty of classes on site, forming an important part of neighbourhood life today.

Address Taxingegränd 10, 16364 Stockholm-Tensta | Public transport Tensta (T-bana 10) |
Opening times Mon 11am–9pm, Tue–Fri 11am–6pm, Sat, Sun 12 midday–5pm | Tip
A bit more than one kilometre away, the Spånga kyrka stands in the Spånga kyrkväg.
Surrounded by modern buildings, the 12th-century church stands as a relic from a bygone
era. Don't miss the sun dial on the outer facade and the medieval frescos inside.

101__ The Textile Centre

Paradise for amateur and professional fashion designers

Bales of fabric are stored everywhere – piled up on the tables and jostling for space on the extensive shelving. In the "Textilcentrum" all kinds of fabric – from shiny silk to robust woollen material – are sold across an area of 1200 square metres. There are also zips in all colours and finishes, buttons, clasps and braids.

The small shop opened in 1960, when various fabric manufacturers had to close. The Textilcentrum bought the remainders, offering them for sale in a tiny shop around the corner from today's company headquarters. On the first day there was already an overwhelming demand with a long queue forming outside the shop despite little publicity.

Over the following years 15 fabric and haberdashery shops closed down in the area, leaving the Textilcentrum with a monopoly. Soon there wasn't enough space and the business moved into larger premises, which soon after became too small again. In the 1970s, school performances resulted in a strong increase in turnover. And when demand from that sector declined, theatre, as well as film and TV productions took their place. In the early 1990s the business moved into the space it occupies today.

Since the success of Liv Ulmann's film "Kristin Lavransdattir", set in the Middle Ages, a new clientele has been storming the Textilcentrum: fans of "LARP", a live role play where participants take on fantasy roles and improvise.

These days, demand for fabrics suitable for medieval or fantasy costumes has increased to the point that the shop's homepage has set up a separate section for LARP fans. But regular amateur dressmakers are equally welcome. The place is particularly popular with female school leavers preferring to sew the dress for their school prom themselves.

Address Järnvägsgatan 56, 17235 Stockholm-Sundbyberg | Public transport Duvbo
(T-bana 10); Fredsgatan (bus 504) | Opening times Mon–Fri 9.30am–6pm,
Sat 10am–3pm | Tip Even if the selection in the first room is already overwhelming,
the fascination continues in the rear part. Many customers don't realise that the door
at the end of the shop opens to reveal shelves upon shelves laden with fabrics.

102_ Trädgården under Bron
Let's party

You're likely to feel a little like Alice in Wonderland here. In the area below and between the tall concrete pillars of the Skanstull Bridge, visitors can spend entertaining leisure time against an extremely creative and lovingly designed backdrop. At the entrance brightly painted tin flowers – as tall as a man – greet the visitor. Set between two of the bridge's pillars, the bright green house with windows and a chimney is an art project. Below, various vintage sofas covered with green or colourfully patterned velvet are flanked by an orderly row of orange-coloured plastic lampshades from the 1970s.

Between May and September, the "Trädgården under bron" stages hip open-air party nights. The place rocks until the wee hours. The stage regularly welcomes bands but drama and performances are put on too.

And there is much more going on: play a round of boule with friends in a dedicated area, stocking up on cool drinks at a camper van. The cocktail bar serves fine long drinks with or without alcohol. The ambience is more elegant here, and – it goes without saying – prices a little higher. More basic fare available from the Caravan Bar includes burgers and beers. On Fridays and Saturdays, they put on dance music from funk and independent to house and other electronic sounds. In the "Club", people listen to slightly harder beats, and at the "Red House", hip hop and R&B are the name of the dancing game. In the "Hothouse" restaurant, diners enjoy dishes made with organic ingredients. Beans, herbs and salad are harvested at the neighbouring Urban Farming project "Garden on Rails" (see page 82). Those who wish to can play a round of table tennis between courses.

In winter the party carries on in the former customs house under the bridge: in the "Under Bron" nightclub that is spread across two storeys.

Address Hammarby slussväg 2, 11860 Stockholm-Södermalm www.tradgarden.com | Public transport Skanstull (T-bana 17, 18, 19; bus 3, 4, 55, 74, 94, 96, 164, 193–195, 791, 794) | Opening times Mon, Tue 5pm–1am, Wed–Fri 5pm–3am, Sat 12 noon–3pm | Tip "Yardie" at Fimlångsvägen 50 is Sweden's first Jamaican snack bar; the range of dishes includes vegetarian fare.

103 The Traneberg Bridge
A new lease of life for old glory

In 1934 this was the pride of the nation. In the presence of 6000 people, Gustaf VI Adolf inaugurated the Tranebergsbro. At the time, the parallel concrete arches of 181 metres length, spanning the Tranebergssund, were considered the longest in the world. The bridge, measuring 461 metres/1512 feet, connects Kungsholmen Island with the western suburb of Bromma, which at the time already included the garden town of Äppelviken, as well as Traneberg and Abrahamsberg with its multi-storey tenant blocks.

As early as 1787 Gustav III had a floating bridge constructed here to create a new access to Drottningholm. That bridge was twice replaced by more modern constructions. The predecessor of the Tranebergsbro, able to support a tram, had to go, as it lacked the capacity for traffic from the heavily populated western suburbs. It took only three years to construct the impressive concrete deck arch bridge by architect Paul Hedqvist. It is shared by bikers, pedestrians, cars, trams and nowadays the underground.

In the decades that followed the city purchased large areas in the west, creating new residential areas such as Hässelby or Blackeberg on green land.

The Tranebergsbro formed the vital link connecting all those places. Over the years, wear and tear had an impact on the old lady, with gritting salt in winter compounding it. Once so proud, the construction developed dangerous fissures and was suffering from old age.

Between 1999 and 2005 the Tranebergsbro was thoroughly refurbished and extended by a third arch.

The view is particularly impressive from the western side. Wandering among the pillars of the bridge allows you to admire the three arches from below. For an even better view wait for the Tranebergssund to freeze over.

Address Tranebergsstrand, 16745 Stockholm-Bromma | Public transport Tranebergsslingan (bus 114) | Tip There is a fine walk (of some three kilometres/a little under 2 miles) from the bridge. Follow Tranebergsvägen underneath the structure, which leads into Tranebergsstrand. At "Sjöpaviliong" turn left into Alviksstrand, continue along the waterfront, through forest and villa areas to the Bromma Marine Service. There, turn right into the Flädermorsbacken, left into the Sunnerdahlsvägen, right into Andersens väg. The end point is the tram stop "Smedslätten".

104_ The Tumba Bruksmuseum
Where the Swedish krona are made

Tumba is a place with a proud tradition. For over 250 years Sweden's bank notes have been manufactured here. Protected by a tall fence, today's printing press lies next to its predecessor. A large part of the workshops and residential homes still exist and today serve as a museum.

The first means of payment made from paper made its appearance as early as 1661. It was considered practical, but on the other hand was easy to forge, as it was printed on regular paper. Which is why Sweden's Riksbank decided in 1755 to introduce special banknotes and establish a secret production site for the purpose. The isolated Hof Tumba seemed to be the perfect candidate. From here, it was easy to transport the monies into the city by boat. Moreover, there was already a mill on the estate. Only the production of the banknotes seemed at first to be beset by difficulties.

As the best papermakers of the era hailed from the Netherlands, the Dutch brothers Mulder were invited to set up operations. However, the know-how of manufacturing paper was subject to the highest secrecy and passing on this knowledge was strictly prohibited. Jan Mulder was imprisoned, only his brother Erasmus made it to Tumba following a dramatic escape in 1758. One year later he was to print the first banknote.

In the decades that followed, the facility came to employ over 300 staff, a doctor and a teacher. In 1770 it was Tumba that opened the first school in the region. Later, a fire fighting department was added, a band and a sports club.

The heart and soul of Tumba is paper master Gunnar Ståhl, who worked here up until 1999. He is the last of his trade in Stockholm. When the old man bends over the large wooden vats and demonstrates with passion and dedication how paper is made by hand and how watermarks are created, or vividly explains how printing plates are crafted, the old works come to life once again.

Address Sven Palmes väg 2, 14743 Tumba, www.tumbabruksmuseum.se | **Public transport** Commuter train to Södertälje, stop Tumba; bus 725, 791, stop Tumbabruksmuseum | **Opening times** Sept–Apr Sat–Sun 11am –4pm, May–Aug Tue–Sun 11am–4pm | **Tip** We recommend taking part in a guided tour through the museum. Lasting 1.5 hours, it is only run in Swedish. However, groups of up to 25 people may book a tour in English (ring in advance, tel. +468/51955346).

105_The Tunnelbana Station Kungsträdgården

A unique ecosystem

Most travellers know the T-bana station Kungsträdgården for its impressive artistic design, with a cleverly illuminated ensemble of neo-classical pillars and statues standing in front of the bare rock wall. Visitors with a keen eye will notice that the rock is partly covered with a green-violet vegetal layer.

Artist Ulrik Samuelson wanted to create a subterranean garden that formed one entity with its surroundings. He ultimately succeeded to a far greater extent than he could ever have anticipated. Researchers with the Natural History Museum are besides themselves with joy, as a unique ecosystem has materialised within the artwork. The pillow moss growing here has only been found to thrive in hothouses in Stockholm since the 1930s and otherwise only flourishes on Öland and Gotland.

More exciting than this is the fact that a two-millimetre dwarf spider has settled down here in an environment that is available nowhere else in other parts of Sweden. Its natural habitat are caves, pits and catacombs in southern Europe. The insect must have hitched a ride on one of the machines used for the construction of the T-bana station in 1977.

But that's not all: Kungsträdgården is the only station where violet, turquoise and dark-green salt deposits have formed. Water is continuously dripping from the ceiling. The result is the beginning of a dripstone cave. Another mystery, as the cave consists of granite, and dripstone caves normally form on limestone or marble. Which is why in Sweden they're only found on Gotland and in the mountains. The excitement was so great that the station was closed for a while in 2012 to allow the researchers to take numerous samples. Who knows what else they might find?

Address Kungsträdgården T-bana, 11147 Stockholm-Norrmalm | Public transport Kungsträdgården (T-bana 10, 11) | Tip Nearby, the first private street in Stockholm, Wahrendorffsgatan, was financed by the restaurateur William Davidson and Baron Martin von Wahrendorff, who without hesitating named the street after himself. In 1912 the Wahrendorff house made way for a bank building, the same year the street took the Baron's name as its official designation.

106_Ugglan Boule & Bar

A subterranean playground for adults

If you manage to open the heavy iron door below the simple sign saying "Boule", you will be standing in front of a row of provisional rent-a-loos. Beyond that, a steep steel staircase leads down into a kind of concrete bunker. Those who dare climb down land in a large unique games paradise for adults.

Four young men are playing a round of boule on a nicely raked gravel track. Painted on the wall behind the young people, a large colourful VW bus looks so inviting that you want to board it straight away. This is the work of Polish art students who have left their mark everywhere on the crude concrete walls with large-scale paintings. Hanging on the other side of the room are dartboards and on the concrete pillars small slide rules to keep track of the score. Comfy leather armchairs invite players to chill between rounds. There is a pinball machine in a corner with two young women playing a round of pingpong in front of it. Everything looks a bit as if one had ended up in a private basement leisure room.

In a larger room two elderly couples are challenging each other at another boule rink. Behind them a group of players is taking a break at a long bar counter.

A billiards, air hockey and table football tables stand between colourful concrete pillars. They say basketball hoops will soon be hanging there too. And those who prefer to play sitting down have countless boardgames to choose from.

In a small room a band is rehearsing for their live performance. Players can recover here from their competitive activities listening to some music. And when the hunger pangs strike, the restaurant area offers fortifying snacks.

In a nutshell: visitors will find everything they need for a varied games evening with a difference. On short dark days during the cold season this is a tried and tested remedy for winter depressions.

Address Närkesgatan 6, 11640 Stockholm-Södermalm | Public transport Närkesgatan (bus 59) | Tip A few houses further on the "Fietsfabriek" manufactures custom-made, high-quality bicycles, which like the Dutch models have large transport boxes.

107 __ The Uggleviken Reservoir
A temple to water, fashion and art

Uggleviken was once the name of a lake forming part of the Norra Djurgården district. All that is left today is a marshy area overgrown with alders. This is one of the most interesting natural habitats in Stockholm, home to extremely rare species of plants and birds.

Standing like a temple amidst this forest area, the Uggleviken water reservoir was designed by well-known Swedish architect Paul Hedqvist. The functionalist building from 1935 was actually inspired by Athen's Parthenon. With a capacity of 18,000 cubic metres, the tank is supported by 64 pillars twelve metres/nearly 40 feet high.

The impact of the impressive building is heightened by the fact that it stands on a mound surrounded by trees. No other building detracts from the sight.

In 1989 this very special ambience inspired the artist couple Reich+Szyber to an arts performance. Entitled "Beautiful Sadness", it involved 27 dancers spending three nights suspended from the concrete pillars six metres above the ground. A pianist accompanied the performance with romantic 19th-century piano music. In 2007, the Filippa K fashion chain used the original setting for the presentation of its new summer collection. The pillars were sandblasted for the event so the water temple peaks out even more conspicuously now from amongst the trees.

Paul Hedqvist did not only set high standards in architecture, but also in terms of technology. The Uggleviken reservoir was the first water tank without heat insulation. Calculations had predicted that with a quantity of water that big even if outside temperatures fell beneath 25 degrees below zero, the temperature within the tank would only go down by a few tenths of a grade. In the cold winters of the early 1940s those calculations turned out to be correct. The system remains in use to this day and the reservoir is one of the largest in Stockholm.

Address Between Uggleviksvägen and Norra Fiskartorpsvägen, 11542 Stockholm-Norra Djurgården | Public transport Bus 55, stop Tennis stadion | Tip The Fiskartorp Hopparbacke on Björnnäsbacken Street was Stockholm's first ski jump in 1890. Because of its steep angle and as it ended on the lake, it was also called the Suicide Jump.

108__Under the Väster Bridge

Scale the heights of cool

After visiting the area underneath Lilla Västerbro, the meaning of the expression "urban feeling" becomes perfectly clear. Between the mighty concrete pillars supporting the bridge that leads traffic over Rålambshovs Park, visitors reach a sports ground. There is a 100-metre track, a long-jump pit and various basketball hoops. A mother is racing her tiny tot over the track and the local youth are playing a round of basketball among the hoops.

A skatepark which was built under the bridge on the initiative of the Stockholm Subsurfers 2010 is at the other end. Those visiting on a fine day need strong nerves, as a spectator in particular.

With its dips and pits of varying depth and width, the run is suitable for both beginners and professionals. Beginners are definitely in the majority here and some look as if they've only just learned to walk.

The youngest whizz down the ramps with little scooters instead of skateboards, which seems no less breathtaking. A little girl, her blonde locks trying to escape the confines of her helmet rolls down a steep incline with not a care in the world and up again the other side. The little boy with her is certainly not going to stay behind, rushes after her and also arrives safe and sound. Guardian angels have a full-time job here.

A few expert skateboarders come together under the bridge, too. They can be recognised by the fact that they eschew helmets in favour of cool woolly hats. The odd one is already growing a beard. Scooters are still en vogue with a few of this older crowd; a few adolescents can be seen executing acrobatic tricks with them too. What is important here is to pause between runs, adopt a cool poise, enjoy the moment of glory and check who's watching.

Address Rålambshovsparken, 11235 Stockholm-Kungsholmen | **Public transport** Thorildsplan (T-bana 17, 18, 19); Västerbroplan (bus 1, 4, 40, 62, 77, 91, 94, 151, 153, 726, 743, 745) | **Tip** Within sight of the sports grounds, the white concrete building standing on a lawn with a pointed roof resembling a sunroof is actually a sculpture by artist Elli Hemberg that represents a butterfly.

109___The Valand Bakery
Where less is more

The Valand Bakery forms a pleasant counterpart to modern cafés with their huge range of sandwiches, bagels, muffins and various cream tarts. The pretty glass display case features only a few select pastries and filled rolls, neatly arranged. Neither latte macchiato nor a cappuccino is offered here; regular filter coffee is kept warm in a simple glass pot on a hot plate.

The furnishings, too, speak of simplicity. Stellan Åström, who has been running the café for nearly 60 years now with his wife Magdalena, originally from Germany, designed them himself. Nothing has been changed here since the shop opened in 1954. The beautiful teak walls are very well preserved, as are the mirror-backed shelves with the glasses sparkling in front and the compartments filled with lemonade bottles lined up like soldiers in a row. The wooden latticework partition separating the sales room from the L-shaped café area is a reminder of a past long gone.

Only the plain tables show the wear and tear of the ages; it is easy to tell that countless people have eaten their cake off them, but this only serves to increase their charm. Next to the entrance there is one particular detail that sticks out: an old telephone with a dial and a sign below admonishing callers to limit their conversation to three minutes.

In the past, when there were plenty of cinemas in the area the café would stay open until eleven at night and the Åströms employed several staff.

Today, the elderly couple runs the place on their own. Alongside faithful regulars, some of whom were already enjoying Madalena's tartlets in the 1950s, their guests include young people from the neighbourhood, artists and students. Prepared to forego their customary trendy latte for the special atmosphere here they prefer to surf the web on their laptops at Valand's instead.

Address Surbrunnsgatan 48, 11348 Stockholm-Vasastan | Public transport Odenplan
(T-bana 17, 18, 19) | Opening times Mon–Fri 8am–7pm, Sat 9am–5pm | Tip At
Drottninggatan 120 the old observatory is located atop a 42m/138-feet hill, a good
spot to enjoy fine views of the city. Café "Himlavalvet" serves home-made lilac berry
juice, bread and fresh waffles.

110_Vinterviken
Where Alfred Nobel let rip

Surrounded by walking trails, the lake occupies a peaceful position amidst a little forest. Children are bathing on one side of the bay, on the other a loved-up couple is out on a stroll. Beyond them is the gaping entrance to a concrete tunnel in the rocks, which seems a little out of place here. This is a reminder that things weren't always that quiet here. Around the lake and the adjacent area was once home to Alfred Nobel's dynamite factory, where he let rip from time to time.

Once Nobel's laboratory on Södermalm had exploded in 1864, he was no longer allowed to carry out his experiments within Stockholm. Whereupon he purchased the Vinterviken Estate. The narrow valley, protected on each side by wooded rocks, seems a perfect choice.

After inventing dynamite in 1866, Alfred Nobel erected factories, blasting pits and storage facilities. On Lake Mälar, a port was built to ship the dangerous goods, using a narrow-gauge railway to get them waterborne. In neighbouring Mörtviken Bay, Nobel had flats built for his workers, at a safe distance from the factory. Just how dangerous producing dynamite was revealed itself in 1868, when 14 workers died in an explosion in the lab. In 1874, another accident claimed twelve more lives. In 1921 the "Nitro Nobel AB" stopped the manufacture of dynamite in Vinterviken, but carried on using the area for storage. Trial blasts were still carried out here up to 1988.

Today Vinterviken belongs to the city, which rehabilitated the area in 1998, when Stockholm was Capital of Culture. A sculpture park was laid out and a few buildings restored, the lab and a storage facility amongst them. However, the production of dynamite left invisible traces too. As recently as 2011 it was found that the soil had an above-average concentration of arsenic and lead.

Address Vinterviksvägen, 11765 Stockholm-Hägersten | Public transport Aspudden (T-bana 13); Mörtviken (bus 133) | Tip Nobel's former sulphur factory at Vinterviksvägen 60 now houses the pretty café and events venue "Vinterviken".

111 The YK-Haus

A house for working couples with children

The eight-storey cream-coloured residential block doesn't stick out much in between the other blocks of tenant flats so common in this part of Östermalm. Every floor has three balconies, with small green tiles on the side.

1960s? 1970s? Wrong. This historic building was built in the 1930s and is one of the few "Collective Houses" that were created in Stockholm at that time. The idea was to create places where ideas for modern community life could be realised.

The Club of Working Women (Yrkeskvinnors Klubb), or YK for short, commissioned Swedish architect Albin Stark and his young colleague Hillevi Svedberg in 1939 to build the YK House.

The residential units were intended for working couples with children. Every floor had a small apartment for the cleaning staff that looked after household chores and laundry. The idea was that not every woman was equally suited for housework and that there was a need for trained staff. The same went for the education of the children who were supervised on the ground floor in a larger room with access to the courtyard. There was also a shared gymnastics hall.

To spare the working parents the task of having to cook in the evenings, there was a shared kitchen as well as a restaurant on the ground floor, where the families were able to dine in the company of other residents. If they wanted to be on their own they just ordered food in the kitchen and had it sent via the dumb waiter to their floor.

A lovely plan. Unfortunately the project failed. Many couples separated. Others stayed when the children had long left the nest.

At some point the functional layout just no longer fitted the tenants' requirements. Which is why today it is a regular residential house.

Address Furusundsgatan 9, 11537 Stockholm-Östermalm | Public transport Gärdet (T-bana 13; bus 1 and 91) | Tip The ground floor houses the Chinese restaurant "ShanghaiGourmet", offering excellent and authentic Chinese cuisine. The dumb waiter in the kitchen is still the original one and is occasionally used too.

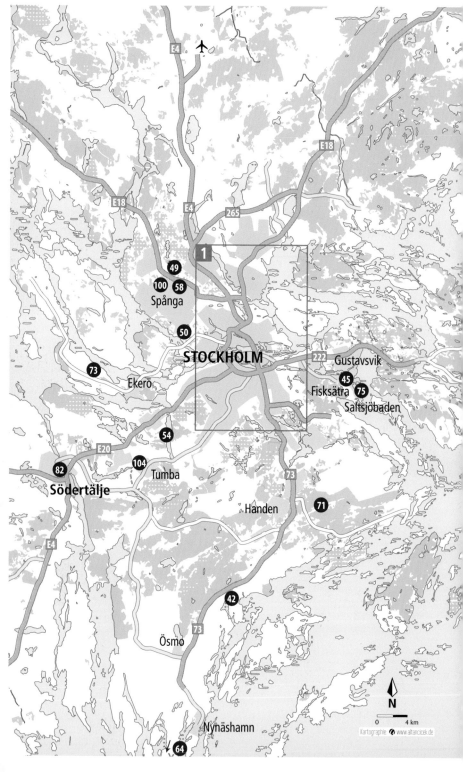

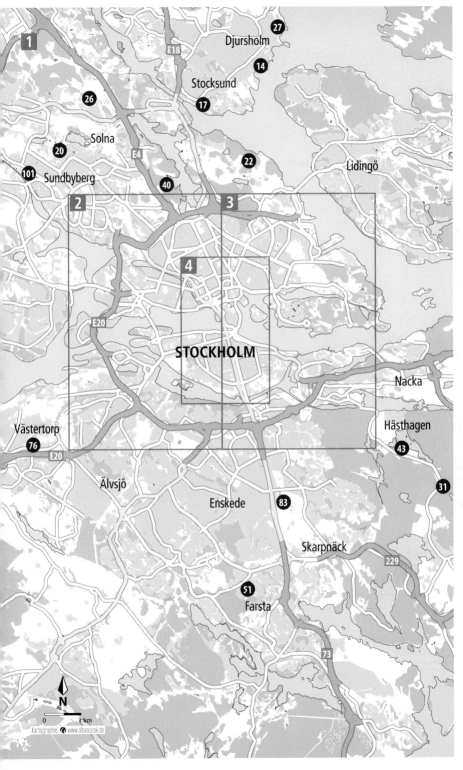

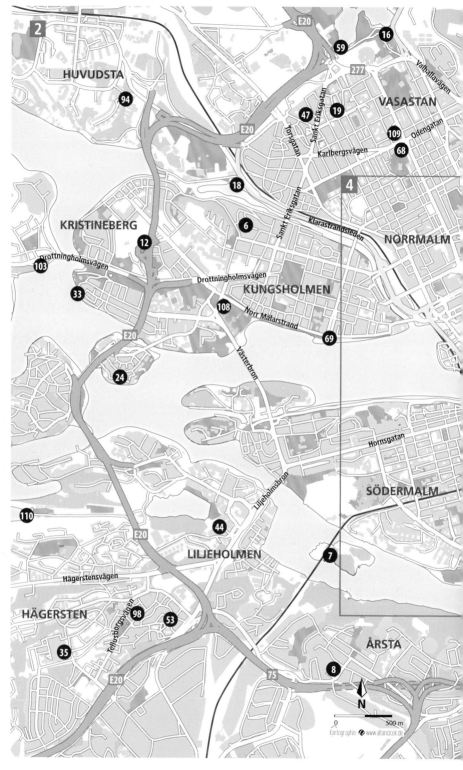

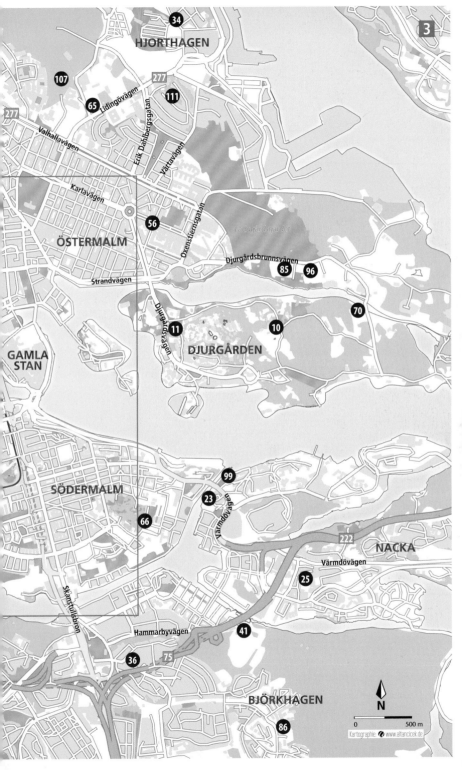

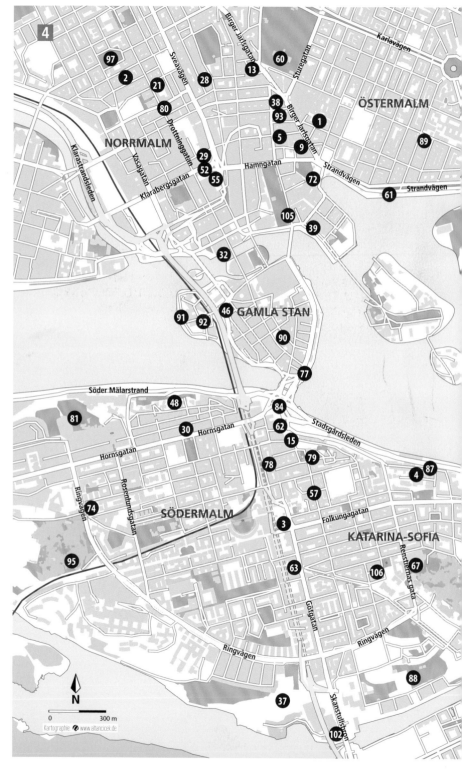

Lucia Jay von Seldeneck,
Carolin Huder, Verena Eidel
**111 PLACES IN BERLIN
THAT YOU SHOULDN'T MISS**
ISBN 978-3-95451-208-9

Rüdiger Liedtke
**111 PLACES IN MUNICH
THAT YOU SHOULDN'T MISS**
ISBN 978-3-95451-222-5

Rike Wolf
**111 PLACES IN HAMBURG
THAT YOU SHOULDN'T MISS**
ISBN 978-3-95451-234-8

Paul Kohl
**111 PLACES IN BERLIN
ON THE TRAIL OF THE NAZIS**
ISBN 978-3-95451-323-9

John Sykes
**111 PLACES IN LONDON
THAT YOU SHOULDN'T MISS**
ISBN 978-3-95451-346-8

Dirk Engelhardt
**111 PLACES IN BARCELONA
THAT YOU MUST NOT MISS**
ISBN 978-3-95451-353-6

Peter Eickhoff
**111 PLACES IN VIENNA
THAT YOU SHOULDN'T MISS**
ISBN 978-3-95451-206-5

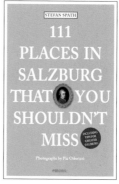

Stefan Spath
**111 PLACES IN SALZBURG
THAT YOU SHOULDN'T MISS**
ISBN 978-3-95451-230-0

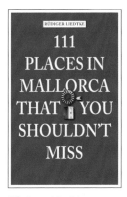

Rüdiger Liedtke
**111 PLACES ON MALLORCA
THAT YOU SHOULDN'T MISS**
ISBN 978-3-95451-281-2

Marcus X. Schmid
**111 PLACES IN ISTANBUL
THAT YOU MUST NOT MISS**
ISBN 978-3-95451-423-6

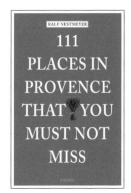

Ralf Nestmeyer
**111 PLACES IN PROVENCE
THAT YOU MUST NOT MISS**
ISBN 978-3-95451-422-9

We would like to thank all the staff at Emons for being great to work with; special thanks for practical support, unflagging commitment and helpful tips also go to: Anna Falk, Lasse Gunnarsson, Lasse Gustafson, Gunilla Kjellberg, Tina Klietz, Maria Jonsson, Jordan Lane, Per Öhmann, Beatrice Orlandi and Joel, Lotta Polbring, Maire Roosmann, Bettina Schubert, Claudette Sinn, Katja Sinn and her friends, Agneta Skoglar, Lena Thalin, Susanne Vadström, Marlena Wulf.

We'd like to extend our thanks to the Bröcker, Steinkuhl-Schwegmann and Schröder families for their moral support, as well as to Stefan Schubert and to all our friends!

Christiane Bröcker
Research

In 2004 Christiane Bröcker left Hamburg for Stockholm, for professional reasons, and for one year – that was the plan anyway. Yet she keeps making new and unusual discoveries in this fascinating city on a daily basis, experiencing surprises and eccentric incidents, as well as meeting interesting people. And for as long as that stays this way, she will stay too. For individual and original tours of the city see: www.stockholm-anders.com

Babette Schröder
Texts and photos

Babette Schröder has worked as a freelance journalist and producer, developing TV films and series, and founding her own film production company. Today, her work includes translating English and French-language literature from her Hamburg base. The common denominator in all of this: Babette loves to work with and hunt down good stories.